Interest-Based Barga
A User's Guide

Jerome T. Barrett and John O'Dowd

BOOKS

Trevet Grange, Dunshaughlin, Co. Meath, Ireland.

Note for Librarians: A cataloguing record for this book is available from Library and Archives
Canada at www.collectionscanada.ca/amicus/index-e.html
ISBN 1-4120-6318-3

*Printed in Victoria, BC, Canada. Printed on paper with minimum 30% recycled fibre. Trafford's print shop
runs on "green energy" from solar, wind and other environmentally-friendly power sources.*

TRAFFORD

Offices in Canada, USA, Ireland and UK
This book was published *on-demand* in cooperation with Trafford Publishing. On-demand
publishing is a unique process and service of making a book available for retail sale to the
public taking advantage of on-demand manufacturing and Internet marketing. On-demand
publishing includes promotions, retail sales, manufacturing, order fulfilment, accounting and
collecting royalties on behalf of the author.

Book sales for North America and international:
Trafford Publishing, 6E–2333 Government St.,
Victoria, BC v8t 4p4 CANADA
phone 250 383 6864 (toll-free 1 888 232 4444)
fax 250 383 6804; email to orders@trafford.com
Book sales in Europe:
Trafford Publishing (uk) Ltd., Enterprise House, Wistaston Road Business Centre,
Wistaston Road, Crewe, Cheshire cw2 7rp UNITED KINGDOM
phone 01270 251 396 (local rate 0845 230 9601)
facsimile 01270 254 983; orders.uk@trafford.com
Order online at:
trafford.com/05-1229

10 9 8 7 6 5 4 3 2

Interest-Based Bargaining

TABLE OF CONTENTS

Acknowledgments   vii

Authors   ix

1. Introduction   1

2. From Adversarial Bargaining to Partnership   12

3. Interest-Based Bargaining   31

4. Defining Key Interest-Based Bargaining Terms   51

5. The Interest-Based Bargaining Sequence   62

6. Tools, Techniques and Processes   90

7. U.S. Experience with IBB   104

8. Conclusion   123

Glossary of Key Terms   129

References   132

ACKNOWLEDGMENTS

Jerry Barrett and John O'Dowd are very grateful for the generous support of the Labour Relations Commission and its Chief Executive Kieran Mulvey.

Jerry Barrett writes: I am grateful to the hundreds of labour and management participants in my training or facilitation sessions because they showed me how difficult it is to switch to IBB.

My thanks to the many FMCS mediators with whom I discussed my P.A.S.T. model as I tried to help them overcome their attachment to traditional bargaining. Some FMCS mediators saw the merits of IBB very early.

Thanks, therefore, to Lou Manchise for his early encouragement when P.A.S.T. was just a thought. Years later, Lou persuaded FMCS to give me the Buckeye Award for my efforts. Thanks also to Floyd Wood who lined up several labour-management pairs for me to test out my IBB training programme in 1989, and for acknowledging in his foreword to my 1998 book my help in getting FMCS started with IBB. Thanks also to mediator Barbara Wood who facilitated the first IBB case with NAVCOM and two unions, while I watched, took notes, offered advice and learned a lot about improving the process.

Former FMCS mediator John Stepp earned by thanks for giving me the opportunity to develop my approach to IBB while he headed the Bureau of Labour-Management and Cooperative Programmes in the Labour Department.

Finally, my thanks to John O'Dowd who sent me an email over a year ago, which I almost didn't open, asking me where he could get a copy of my IBB book. After I sent him one, an enjoyable collaboration resulted in this volume.

John O'Dowd writes: Jeanne Frank, FMCS Commissioner in Minneapolis-StPaul, first introduced me to interest-based bargaining and I have enjoyed many conversations with her around this subject. I would like to thank several colleagues and friends for discussions over the years on management-union relationships and organisational change: Tim Hastings, JJ O'Dwyer, Tom McGuinness, Blair Horan, Matt Merrigan, Aine O'Neill, Tom Gormley, John McAdam, Maurice Fines, Ger McDonnell, John O'Halloran, John Dowling, Isobel Butler, Gerry O'Sullivan, Jean Cullinane, Una O'Neill, Bill Roche, and Tom Murphy.

Colleagues from the USA and Canada whom I have learned from are Brian Rius, Abby Yanow, Doug Wylie, Michael Gaffney, Susan Wasstrom, and Debbie Friedman.

Colleagues who have provided insights into the adoption of IBB include Seosamh O Maollalai, Jerome Forde, Donal Wylie, Liz White, Lesley Hewson, Karen Lodge, Breege Kelly, Damien Mullarkey, Denis Rohan, Dolores Geary, John Kavanagh and Jean Curran. Nicky Ryan of Eircom provided invaluable information on interest-based problem solving in that company.

Avalon Print & Design did the book layout and design and also designed the cover. Cartoons are by Richard Chapman. His website is www.doubt.it and he can be contacted by email at cartoons@doubt.it.

Aine O'Neill read the full typescript and commented on it. Karen Scolard provided help with the text in the early stages. Tom Reilly of Trafford Books provided invaluable technical help.

Finally, my thanks to Jerry Barrett who generously agreed to allow his U.S. books on IBB to form the basis of this one.

My input to the book is dedicated to Aine, Fintan and Matthew.

THE AUTHORS

JEROME T. BARRETT

Jerome T. Barrett began his mediation career in the early 1960s as a Minnesota State labour conciliator in St. Paul, following several years with the National Labour Relations Board in Detroit. He continued his mediation career with the Federal Mediation and Conciliation Service (FMCS) in Washington, D.C., Chicago, and Milwaukee.

By the late 1960s, as campus and community violence gained everyone's attention, he published several articles explaining how civil rights and antiwar disputants could use the labour-management model to resolve their disputes peacefully.

In 1969, after five years as a federal mediator, he joined the newly created National Centre for Dispute Settlement to mediate civil rights, campus, and community disputes. As union organising of public employees increased in the early 1970s, Barrett joined the Department of Labour to head a new office providing advice to state and local governments and their unions on establishing procedures for resolving disputes. During that period, he wrote extensively about that rapidly developing field.

In 1973, he returned to FMCS to head the newly created Office of Technical Assistance to manage mediator training, preventive mediation, and the start of FMCS work outside the labour-management field. In the early 1980s, he left FMCS to teach labour relations at Northern Kentucky University and to complete his doctoral degree in human resource development with a dissertation on the history of joint labour-management training with a focus on FMCS and its predecessor, the U.S. Conciliation Service. While teaching, Barrett began an arbitration practice and did overseas consulting on labour relations and ADR. He would eventually work in twenty-four countries.

His other education includes a B.A. from the College of St. Thomas and an M.A. from the University of Minnesota. In the mid-1980s, he returned to the Department of Labour's Bureau of Labour Management and Cooperative Programmes, where he developed the Partners in Change Programme for FMCS to assist labour and management in enhancing their cooperative efforts.

He also created an interest-based bargaining programme called P.A.S.T. and an accompanying training programme, which he has since used hundreds of times. He introduced FMCS mediators to interest-based bargaining (IBB) with his P.A.S.T. training model, helping to start what is now an extensive FMCS programme.

Since leaving the government in 1988, Barrett has written, arbitrated, trained, and facilitated. He has written two books on IBB and produced an IBB video with the University of Wisconsin. In 2004, he wrote *A History of Alternative Dispute Resolution: The Story of a Political, Cultural, and Social Movement,* which was published by Jossey Bass.

He serves as historian of the Society of Professionals in Dispute Resolution and FMCS. For the past three years, he has written an ADR history column for the ACResolution quarterly magazine. For the past seven years, he has been an elected school board member in Falls Church, Virginia, where he lives with his wife, Rose. They have five sons and five grandchildren.

JOHN O'DOWD

John O'Dowd is a consultant and facilitator specialising in industrial and employee relations. Much of his work lies in helping employers and trade unions to work together to develop better industrial relations and to develop effective ways of handling change together. Through John O'Dowd Consultants Ltd he provides a range of consulting, training, facilitation and mediation services to employers and trade unions. His website is www.johnodowd.com. He brings to his work a deep practical and theoretical understanding of industrial relations and organisational change.

From 1997 to 1999 he was Joint Director of the National Centre for Partnership, based in the Department of the Taoiseach. In that role he was responsible for the facilitation of partnerships across the public sector, including health boards, local authorities, commercial state companies, universities, government departments and others. He developed the first standardized training materials for newly formed partnership groups in the public sector. He published *Employee Partnership in Ireland* (Oak Tree Press) in 1998.

He was Assistant General Secretary of the Association of Secondary Teachers Ireland from 1980 to 1988. He was General Secretary, Civil and Public Service Union from 1988 to 1997. During that time he was also a member of the Executive Council of the Irish Congress of Trade Unions and took part in the negotiation of national programmes.

He is a graduate of University College Dublin (UCD). He has a BA in

English and French, a Higher Diploma in Education, and holds an MBA from the Open University Business School. His is currently an Associate Fellow of the Michael Smurfit Graduate School of Business, UCD, where he is researching a doctorate on workplace partnership in the private sector. He teaches negotiation skills to MBS students in UCD.

- 1 -

INTRODUCTION

Markets and technologies are moving faster than at any time before. Enterprises regard competitive advantage as temporary. To stop falling behind competitors, private and public enterprises are striving to achieve high levels of internal flexibility, problem solving and creativity.
    A Quality Shift in Employment Relations: Labour Relations Commission Statement of Strategy 2005-2007.

BACKGROUND

ADVERSARIAL COLLECTIVE BARGAINING of the 'them and us' variety has been – and in many cases continues to be - the dominant means of communication between management and trade unions at workplace level in Ireland. Not alone does the settlement of disputes relating to pay, conditions of employment and job security take place this way but frequently the discussion of important organisational changes also takes place through adversarial bargaining. Arrangements that encourage representatives of management and workers to handle issues together outside adversarial collective bargaining have until recently been uncommon.

    Adversarial collective bargaining is both a method for negotiating wages and conditions of employment and a process for setting the broad contours of the 'social contract' at work, i.e. how managers, union representatives and employees are expected to think about and behave towards each other (Walton et al, 1994). Thus within the 'Anglo Saxon' industrial relations tradition associated with the United Kingdom, the USA, and Ireland, among others, it is assumed that that there is a pervasive conflict of interest between management and trade unions on fundamental issues. This in turn supports a short-term, low trust perspective in which the strategies and tactics of each side depend on the changing balance of power between them. This balance of power is influenced by factors such as the economy and the government in power (Bean, 1994). Seen this way, the social contract or overall management-union-employee relationship represents as important an outcome of bargaining as specific agreements on substantive issues.

1

This is not to suggest that all adversarial bargaining is of a 'bare knuckles' type. In most cases, management and unions share a desire to get as much as possible out of the employment relationship (Cooke, 1990). But they also share a desire to bargain, in most situations, in an orderly fashion, i.e. without disputes or disruption, and to reach agreements around which both sides can be reasonably satisfied. In most cases, both management and unions accept the need for voluntary restraint in the use of unilateral power. Bargaining practice, therefore, tends towards a restrained model of adversarialism based on a shared interest in maintaining stable industrial relations (Murphy, 1997). Nevertheless, the system supports a low trust, 'arms length' relationship between managers, union representatives and employees in the workplace.

There was some experimentation in Ireland in the 1970s with new forms of employee and trade union involvement alongside collective bargaining through works councils or works committees. Agendas tended to focus on issues linked to production and social activities (O'Hanlon, 1976). The evidence from the late 1990s, however, was that the incidence of works councils or works committees was only around 21% in organisations of 50 or more employees and the majority of these had been established more than three years previously (Gunnigle et al, 1997). Unlike many other European states, Ireland did not experience statutory approaches to trade union and employee involvement until the Employee Information and Consultation Directive became effective in 2005 (NCPP, 2004 (c)).

Given the historical linkages between Ireland and the United Kingdom it is not surprising that UK industrial relations values and practices should have substantially influenced the conduct of industrial relations in Ireland. Up until the arrival of significant numbers of US multi-nationals in the 1970s, British companies dominated the landscape here and even today their role continues to be very important.

NEW EMPLOYMENT TIMES

Since joining the European Union Ireland's industrial relations landscape has been significantly influenced by wider European developments, in particular by the appeal of the Nordic 'social partnership' approach to industrial relations (Bean, 1994). It has also been significantly influenced by the increasing presence of large US multinationals that have espoused radically different approaches to management-union-employee relations than the traditional adversarial industrial relations-based approach.

2

Introduction

The types of 'human resource management' associated with these companies commonly stress the importance of having a high trust relationship between managers and employees that can support ongoing change and performance improvements in circumstances where employers regard competitive advantage as only temporary and not to be taken for granted. Direct communications with employees, new forms of work organisation such as teams, new reward systems and 'flatter' organisational structures are frequently associated with 'human resource management'.

In many cases US multinationals, as well as Irish companies, reject any role for trade unions, which they characterise as unnecessary 'third parties', and opt for strong managerial control and direct communications with employees on issues affecting them.

There has also been a considerable expansion of and change in the composition of the workforce over the past twenty years (LRC, 2005; NCPP, 2005). The numbers of women and graduates at work has increased enormously. It has been estimated that an additional 300,000 employees with third level qualifications will be needed by 2015 and that by that time one in four people will be employed in knowledge-intensive professions (NCPP, 2005). It has also been estimated that in twenty years time females will form a majority of the best-educated segment of the population and probably will outnumber men in employment (LRC, 2005).

Over this period, there has been a significant decline in employment in traditional industries such as clothing and textiles and others. Furthermore, there has been a major decline in trade union density in the private sector but not in public services. The absolute numbers belonging to a trade union have increased during the past fifteen years but trade union membership has not kept pace with the quite exceptional levels of employment growth over this period (LRC, 2005). At the same time, trade unions retain a significant influence on the character and direction of employment relations in Ireland, not least through their role in the negotiation of successive national programmes.

Since the late 1980s, pay across the economy has been settled through multi-year social partnership agreements involving the government and the national employer and trade union bodies, thus removing pay in most cases from the local collective bargaining agenda. Since 1997 national programmes have also promoted the development at workplace level of 'partnership' arrangements as a means of bringing managers, employees and union representatives together in a more open and cooperative relationship than that associated with adversarial collective bargaining.

Workers' entitlements such as annual leave, maternity leave, equal opportunities, working time, pensions, redundancies etc that were formerly settled through collective bargaining and enshrined in voluntary agreements are now fixed through legislation (Duffy, 2005). According to the Labour Relations Commission (LRC) it is not stretching credibility to talk about a rights-based employment relations system emerging in Ireland (LRC, 2005). Additionally, many of the new procedures for handling disputes now provide for binding outcomes as opposed to negotiated ones (Duffy, 2005). In effect, the scope for adversarial conflict at workplace level around many issues that were contentious in the past has narrowed in recent years. This has led some observers to talk of the 'end of voluntarism' and the gradual reshaping of the parameters of industrial relations in the context of a more law-based system (Duffy, 2005; King, 2005).

In tandem with these developments, Ireland has enjoyed over the past decade significant economic success that has markedly improved the living standards of the majority of people. The country has transformed from a high-tax, high-debt economy with high levels of emigration and unemployment to one that can more or less balance budgets, that has low tax rates and that enjoys net immigration.

CHANGING INDUSTRIAL RELATIONS

Since the 1980s, the workplace industrial relations agenda has been shifting from a union-driven focus on pay and conditions towards a management-driven focus on issues such as continuous improvement, quality, new reward systems, work organisation and job design, new organisational structures etc. This change of emphasis in the bargaining agenda reflects a shift in the 'centre of gravity' of industrial relations in many advanced economies, including Ireland, away from trade unions towards employers (Ferner and Hyman, 1994; Locke et al, 1995).

External pressures on companies generated by an increasingly competitive private sector and governmental and societal pressures on public service organisations have been driving this shift to a management-driven agenda. Indeed, it has been argued of the public services that the drive for modernisation has turned this part of the economy into a major arena for workplace change that will place significant demands on conflict management systems (LRC, 2005).

It also appears now that the traditional low trust, arms length 'social contract' between managers, employees and union representatives is being recast within many organisations. Rather than assuming that there is a pervasive conflict of interest between management and trade unions on fundamental issues, through the series of national programmes since *Partnership 2000* (Government of Ireland, 1997), management and trade unions now explicitly state that organisational success is a common concern they both share. They also state that a less adversarial and more problem solving approach to industrial relations is in the interest of both management and trade unions.

It is clear that in the right conditions, higher levels of trust based on higher levels of involvement can be generated between managers, employees and union representative. Furthermore, it is evident that many parties aspire to having such a relationship. Survey findings from the National Centre for Partnership and Performance (NCPP) show that managers considered building trust between management and unions as salient: one-third considered this to be very important currently while more than half expected it to become very important over the next three years (NCPP, 2004(b)).

In addition, employees who report high levels of consultation around decisions affecting their work are much more likely to be willing to embrace change (NCPP, 2005). There is also evidence that union members want their unions to be more pro-active in cooperating with management and to focus both on pay and conditions and on the future development of the organisation (NCPP, 2005).

This is not to suggest that adversarial collective bargaining has been replaced as the dominant form of communication between management and trade unions in the majority of workplaces. Nor is it to suggest that the only alternative to collective bargaining is high-involvement human resource practices of the partnership kind (Roche and Turner, 1998).

It is, rather, to acknowledge the presence of many alternative approaches that are operating either as replacements for adversarial bargaining or, more commonly, as supplementary channels to it in the unionised sector (Roche, 1996; NCPP, 2005). Our focus is mainly on those organisations that are likely to pursue cooperative management-union strategies including the use of interest-based bargaining.

NEW JOINT MANAGEMENT-UNION ARRANGEMENTS

Given the expanded range of issues that management and unions need to handle together in the workplace it is not surprising that many private companies have now developed 'partnership' structures and tools for the handling of this agenda. In addition, almost all public service employments now have 'partnership committees' of one form or another. These partnership initiatives constitute a range of formal and informal arrangements through which managers, employees and trade union representatives engage with each other outside the formal collective bargaining process on issues of mutual concern, especially issues relating to organisational change and improvement and the quality of working life of employees.

Among the reasons for these innovations, as will be discussed in more detail later, was a sense among managers and union representatives that the traditional adversarial bargaining approach did not lend itself to effective handling of complex issues around organisational change and improvement.

By being involved in such initiatives managers, union representatives and employees have learned new practices and skills on top of those needed to be effective negotiators within the adversarial tradition. A new language of 'jointism' has emerged around terms such as 'partnership', 'common understanding', 'joint ownership of change', 'joint problem solving', 'consensus decision making', 'mutual gains' etc which was unknown to most management and trade union negotiators as recently as the late 1990s.

In addition, many managers, union representatives and employees are now using practices and tools such as flip charts, problem solving techniques, brainstorming, group facilitation, consensus decision making, team building etc to help them to resolve differences and to work together in the design and implementation of organisational changes.

INTEREST-BASED BARGAINING

Interest-based bargaining (IBB) is now beginning to feature to a significant degree among these new practices and skills. Interest-based bargaining (or interest-based problem solving as it is sometimes called) is an approach to collective bargaining or problem solving that is designed to help parties express, understand and build agreements around their underlying interests or concerns and desires. It utilises problem solving tools as a way of avoiding positional conflicts and as a way of achieving better outcomes for all stakeholders. These skills and tools include active listening, converting positions into interests, joint data collection, brainstorming, joint task forces, facilitation, consensus decision making and effective communication with constituents (Fonstad et al, 2004).

Interest-based bargaining is commonly associated with the idea of 'expanding the pie', that is trying to make the pie bigger so that each party can get a bigger slice rather than accepting that the pie has to stay the same size in which case one party's gain has to be at another party's expense. In traditional bargaining it was assumed by managers and also by employees and unions that management had sole responsibility for determining the size of the pie. They did this through decisions relating to organisational performance and output such as operations, marketing, finances and human resources (Cooke, 1990). Within this traditional approach, the role of trade unions was essentially to bargain over how the pie should be shared between management and employees. In many organizations, as seen already, that has now changed with a new and growing role for employees and union representatives in decisions relating to organisational change and improvement.

WHY THIS BOOK?

There are several reasons why we decided to write this book. Firstly, there is evidence of a growing recognition that the capacity to resolve workplace disputes impacts on the quality of the working environment, on organisational performance and on management-employee relations (LRC, 2005; NCPP, 2005). There is also a growing acceptance that the dominant current approaches to dispute resolution are not the only effective ones. In this context there is a developing interest among industrial relations practitioners and policy makers in what have been termed 'alternative dispute resolution' approaches (ADR), including interest-based bargaining.

ADR is a US term for a range of different ways of resolving conflicts other than through legal channels (Barrett and Barrett, 2004). The Labour Relations Commission (LRC) operates a variety of ADR dispute resolution mechanisms including conciliation, mediation and facilitation which are, for the most part, grounded on interest-based bargaining principles.

The LRC has recently set out some key principles underpinning the Commission's approach to the delivery of a flexible conflict prevention and dispute management system (LRC, 2005). These principles emphasise, among other points, the desirability of having a range of different approaches to dispute resolution as opposed to a 'one size fits all' approach, the importance of attempting to solve disputes as close to the point of origin as possible, and the importance of collaborative problem solving and joint action in general between managers, trade unions and employees. The LRC also argues that the context within which dispute resolution takes place is important: systems will work better when mutual trust, good communications, consultation, involvement and participation are features of the workplace.

We consider that the approach to interest-based bargaining or problem solving that we are describing in this book is entirely consistent with these principles. In particular, interest-based bargaining provides opportunities to solve problems close to their point of origin and to involve those most affected by the problems concerned. It also provides opportunities to build relationships where they are poor and to strengthen them where they are already sound by involving managers, union representatives and employees in an intensive form of joint working.

Secondly, there are many organisations in Ireland in which the managements and unions are seeking alternative, more cooperative ways of handling organisational change. These alternative ways are frequently called 'partnership'. In such cases the parties are frequently seeking to develop a 'problem solving' style in place of the traditional adversarial style. In many cases the parties are seeking to 'deepen' the partnership agenda by the handling of issues that are presently handled through adversarial collective bargaining.

One of the reasons, as suggested earlier, for seeking alternatives to adversarial bargaining is because many of the issues now coming on the bargaining agenda like continuous improvement, quality, family friendly policies, human resource policy development, new reward systems, work organisation and job design, new organisational structures etc are not easily addressed using the adversarial model (Cutcher-Gershenfeld, 2003). Such complex issues do not lend themselves to being handled through simple 'for' and 'against' positions. They require considerable teasing out and often provide opportunities and benefits for both management and employees.

The European Union Employee Information and Consultation Directive provides an opportunity to foster partnership-style approaches to managing and anticipating change (NCPP, 2004(c)). If this proves to be the case then managers, union representatives and employees will need processes for the handling of problems that will help to build and sustain cooperative relationships and that will not draw them inadvertently into adversarial bargaining where this is not necessary.

We consider that interest-based bargaining is highly compatible in terms of values, objectives, processes and skills with a partnership approach to organisational change and will, therefore, be of growing interest where managers, trade unions and employees want to develop more cooperative ways of working together.

Thirdly, experience in the USA has shown that major and complex issues including contracts affecting thousands of employees can be successfully negotiated using an interest-based approach. The U.S. experience yields insights into what helps and what hinders the effectiveness of interest-based bargaining, especially in the handling of difficult economic issues such as pay. It will be helpful, hopefully, to capture this practical experience and to bring it to an Irish audience.

Finally, there is no text on interest-based bargaining written in an Irish industrial relations context. Indeed, there are few texts at all specifically devoted to interest based bargaining in the industrial relations context (Walton and McKersie, 1965; Barrett, 1996 and 1998; Weiss, 1996). This is a gap that we thought needed to be filled, as there is evidence now, as already suggested, of a growing interest in this topic.

OUR READERSHIP

This book has been written for those managers, union representatives, employees and students who are interested in finding out more about the interest-based approach to dispute resolution and problem solving. We do not present IBB as an alternative to adversarial bargaining in all situations. Rather the focus will be on situations where it is possible for negotiating parties to work together cooperatively to achieve so-called 'win-win' solutions.

In this context, 'possible' refers not just to the nature of the issues in dispute or the problems to be resolved but also to the prevailing context and especially to the relationships between the parties. IBB, if it is to develop on a widespread basis, is more likely to supplement than replace established collective bargaining methods and grievance handling procedures (Teague, 2004).

We think the following workplace scenarios are good examples of when interest-based bargaining or problem solving might be used:

The management of a local government agency want to contract out grass-cutting services. Costs have escalated in recent years and with newer equipment and lower overheads outside contractors could provide the service at a lower cost. Similar services have been successfully contracted out in the past. The workers are against contracting out but see that it doesn't make sense to simply say 'no'. They said 'no' in the past and it didn't stop it from happening. Give us the same equipment, they say, and we can do the work at the same cost as outside contractors. Give us the financial information and we will show you what we can do. Fine, respond the managers, but your working practices will also have to change in line with private operators if you are going to compete successfully with them.

The management of a plant of a US multi-national have a major concern that to remain competitive and to get investment from their parent company they will need to bring about significant changes in working practices. Relationships with their trade union are reasonably good. At the same time, the bargaining process has proven to be slow and costly in the past. There is a partnership forum and it has done some useful work but mainly around 'soft' issues. The management consider the issues that they want to progress too complex for haggling over in the traditional way. At the same time they are sceptical as to whether the partnership process is strong enough to be able to handle these issues.

A group of nurses complain that they can rarely take holidays when they want to and that the more senior nurses get the first choice at peak holiday periods. Every year this issue leads to bad feelings and to a patched-up temporary solution. The nurses' managers reply that they can't suit everyone because the cost of replacement contract nurses has gone sky high, budgets are tightening and there are strict ceilings on staffing levels. At the same time they acknowledge the problem and see that it is damaging staff morale. The nurses' union wants to avoid one more temporary solution to what is a festering problem for all concerned.

The predominant way of handling these types of situations in Ireland has been adversarial bargaining where representatives of management and trade unions sit across the table from each other to hammer out compromise agreements that, in theory at least, satisfy all parties. All too often, however, there are losers, usually the ones with least power to wield over the others. Or part of the problem may be resolved with other parts being left unresolved 'on the long finger'.

Even where agreements are reached, the bargaining process can and frequently does lead to negative feelings and relationships between employees and managers. The bargaining process may also cause bad feelings among employees and among managers. Sometimes there is conflict that leaves a bitter aftertaste and that affects later interactions.

We argue that the interest-based bargaining approach with its emphasis on understanding the underlying interests of the parties and building solutions around these, and its use of problem solving tools, rather than 'across the table' confrontations, can help the parties to avoid positional conflicts and achieve better outcomes for all stakeholders in the types of situations outlined above.

THE ORGANISATION OF THE BOOK

Chapter 2 provides an overview of traditional adversarial bargaining and the development of workplace partnership in Ireland. Chapter 3 describes the interest-based bargaining approach and contrasts it with adversarial bargaining. Chapter 4 describes in detail the building blocks of interest-based bargaining – issues, positions, interests, options and standards. Chapter 5 describes the five steps in the interest-based bargaining model that is described by us: focussing the issue, identifying interests, developing options, agreeing acceptable standards, and reaching consensus on solutions using these standards. Chapter 6 describes the facilitation assistance and tools needed for interest-based bargaining to work effectively. Chapter 7 discusses the evolution of collective bargaining in the US and recent developments relating to interest-based bargaining which has been used in the USA for more than twenty-five years. Chapter 8 is a conclusion and summary chapter. Finally, we have provided a glossary of the key terms that we use in the book on the assumption that many readers will not be familiar with all of the jargon associated with workplace industrial relations and the different approaches to collective bargaining.

-2-

FROM ADVERSARIAL BARGAINING
TO PARTNERSHIP

'Given the transformation that is occurring in international economic conditions, it seems to be increasingly accepted that the adversarial model no longer provides a viable basis for relations between employees, unions and employers in Ireland'.
   P. Gunnigle and W.K. Roche (1995): New Challenges to Irish Industrial Relations.

INTRODUCTION

IN THIS CHAPTER we discuss how adversarial bargaining works as well as its strengths and limitations. We then discuss the development of workplace partnership against this background. We suggest that many partnership initiatives were influenced by management and trade union perceptions of the limitations of adversarial bargaining. We show that the overall results of partnership have been positive. We also show that many managers and union representatives do not consider the partnership process to be robust enough to handle difficult or contentious issues and that a common fall back is to take such issues into adversarial bargaining.

We suggest that one effective way of handling this difficulty is to adopt an interest-based approach. Interest-based bargaining or problem solving is particularly recommended where the bargaining agenda shows potential for 'win-win' solutions and where management-union relationships are strong enough to support such an approach.

We describe how interest-based bargaining works and contrast it with the adversarial approach. We suggest that interest-based bargaining can be of significant value to parties in organisations that are already working more closely together in partnership or who wish to go down the partnership route. Finally, we give examples of interest-based bargaining in the local government and health sectors in Ireland.

ADVERSARIAL BARGAINING

Adversarial collective bargaining has been given a number of different names: 'distributive bargaining', 'adversarial bargaining', 'positional bargaining', 'traditional bargaining' and 'win-lose bargaining' are the most common. The terms that will be mostly used here are 'positional bargaining' and 'adversarial bargaining'. As already seen, adversarial bargaining has been the traditional approach to the settlement of pay and conditions and workplace change issues in many unionised organisations in Ireland. It is associated with adversarial or 'arms-length' industrial relations of a low trust kind.

Adversarial bargaining developed on the basis of certain assumptions held by employers and trade unions. One was that employers would not willingly grant improvements to pay and conditions of employment and that workers had to fight for these. Related to this was an assumption that the industrial relations procedures existed for the most part to facilitate the processing of trade union claims for improvements in pay and conditions.

Another assumption was that it was the prerogative of management to make decisions about organisational change and that the role of the union was to respond to these decisions in so far as they affected the pay and conditions of members (ICTU, 1995). Finally, there was an assumption that when employers and trade unions failed to persuade the other party to their point of view there would be resort to the power of the union to call a strike or to the power of the employer to impose change unilaterally.

These assumptions underpinned a common view on the part of management and trade unions that it was in both their interests to have 'good industrial relations' and to avoid constant conflict. On this basis, they commonly negotiated procedures for the handling of claims and grievance that provided for negotiation at different levels within organisations and that provided for third party interventions such as mediation and arbitration. These assumptions held sway among employers and trade unions for many years. However, as we saw in Chapter 1, their influence has been in decline in Ireland and elsewhere since the 1980s.

HOW ADVERSARIAL BARGAINING WORKS

In adversarial bargaining the parties arrive at the negotiating table knowing what specific outcomes they want to achieve. The 'rules of the game', however, encourage them to conceal their 'real hands' and to exaggerate, bluff and threaten in order to advance their true positions. In many cases, negative stereotypes tend to dominate each side's opinion of the other, for example the 'militant' shop steward who can never be satisfied and the mean manager who doesn't know how to say 'yes'.

Communications usually take place in a truncated manner. In many instances the negotiating teams address each other through spokespersons and the role of many participants is confined to talking during side sessions or caucus meetings. Members of negotiating teams are expected to 'sing off the same hymn sheet' and not to contradict one another during bargaining sessions.

Typically each party exaggerates its position on an issue in order to pull the settlement closer to their true position, sometimes called a 'bottom line'. Each party develops arguments and advances information to support their own position and to undermine, if not destroy, the other party's position. 'Proposal' and 'demand' are other names for a position. Proposal suggests a somewhat softer connotation, while demand is tougher, but the basic concept is the same, i.e. one party's statement of how to solve the issue separating them from the other party.

In this type of bargaining, negotiators use a ritual of posturing and bluffing to make a series of strategic retreats from their opening positions to reach a settlement. However, the dependence of the process on bluffing and posturing can cause major problems when one party misreads the other side's message or misjudges their own power, when egos get in the way of strategy or when a constituency refuses to abandon a throwaway position at a crucial moment.

These behaviours have important purposes. The exaggeration gives each side the flexibility to get a sense of the other side's intentions and bottom line without revealing their own true position or making a premature commitment that might 'sell them short'.

The bargaining ritual can, and frequently does, become an end in itself with each party expending considerable energy trying to read the other party, trying to send signals, determining whose move it is, bluffing excessively, threatening, attempting to save face, to win at any cost, to sow divisions and to increase hostility, to name just a few standard tactics used in adversarial collective bargaining.

Sometimes parties put positions or demands on the table early on in order to be able to withdraw them and to be seen to be making a significant 'concession' at a later stage. These are often referred to as 'throwaway positions'. Needless to say each party expects a concession from the other side in return for any concession they make themselves.

It is not accidental that adversarial bargaining is so popular. Bargainers are anxious to see how far apart they are, how large the gap is between the sides. Knowledge of the gap size and the negotiators' assessments of the difficulty of bridging the gap helps most negotiators develop their bargaining strategy. Based on the gap size, negotiators assess how much they are willing to move towards the other side's position, and how successful they will be in persuading the other side to move towards their position.

It is also common for lead negotiators on both sides to show their own constituents who may not be present at the bargaining table just how wide the gap may be. This serves at least two purposes. Firstly, it helps to prepare constituents for a settlement that may fall significantly short of their opening demands and positions. Secondly, it prepares constituents for a positive judgment on any reasonable settlement not to mention a positive judgment of the skills and efforts of their negotiators!

These behaviours also demonstrate to constituents that their negotiators have sought to achieve the best possible deal (Cutcher-Gershenfeld, 2003). They show constituents that their negotiators – on whichever side – have not got 'too cosy' with the other side.

POWER AND COLLECTIVE BARGAINING

In adversarial negotiations, power, real or perceived, is usually the main factor that determines the result. Power is the ability to secure another party's agreement on one's own terms. It depends on the cost for that other party of disagreeing on the terms offered as compared to the cost of agreeing them (Chamberlain, 1951). Power comes, in the main, from the environment in which the parties are negotiating, e.g. the condition of the labour market, the overall state of the economy, and the competitive position of a particular firm (Rojot, 1991).

In a given year, if a union has the power to call and maintain an effective work stoppage, it will be able to strongly influence the nature and content of the settlement. Conversely, when unemployment is high, or the employer's market is poor, the settlement will likely favour management. Needless to say, management and trade unions invariably have different perceptions of the environment and in adversarial bargaining they establish their bargaining positions around whatever that perception happens to be.

Because the existence and extent of power is not known, understood or realized until it is actually exercised, the perception of power has great influence. Thus the bargaining power of an employer rests not on that employer's perception of the extent of their power but rather on the trade union perception of the employer's power and vice versa. That fact encourages the parties, as we have already seen, to posture and use tactics that bluff, mislead, exaggerate and disguise. Indeed, adversarial bargaining has been described as a game of managing impressions or manipulating information (Bacharach and Lawler, 1981).

Union membership meetings, strike ballots and results announcements, support of other unions, strike planning, pubic statements etc. are all used to influence the management perception of union power. Management, for its part, has its own tactics for influencing the union's perception of management's power such as selective release of financial information, threats of redundancies, hints that new product development and investment programmes will be stopped, direct appeals or threats to employees, appeals to the wider community, setting of tight deadlines etc.

Bargaining power is also dependent on non-economic environmental factors such as public and media opinion, the political environment, the judicial context, and the technical context (Cooke, 1990; Martin, 1992). It will be seen, for example, in Chapter 7 how political and legislative changes had such dramatic impacts on the relative bargaining power of employers and trade unions in the USA. In Ireland it has not been uncommon for newspaper editorials to lend support to popular groups such as nurses, or for governments faced with disputes involving essential public services to lean towards settlements that favour trade unions, in order to avoid the political costs of interrupted public services.

The technical environment is more relevant in certain cases than in others. For example, a company that operates a twenty-four hour seven days a week production operation and that relies on highly trained employees to maintain production may have less bargaining power than a company that can easily make alternative arrangements to meet customer orders during an industrial dispute. The fact that customers can access services over the Internet may have reduced the bargaining power of employees who traditionally served these customers 'over the counter'. On the other hand, the employees who maintain the Internet service, assuming this is provided in-house, may well have greater bargaining power than in the past.

Finally, there is the question of negotiation skills (Cooke, 1990). If it is the case, as we suggest above, that in negotiations each party is attempting to change the perceptions of the other party regarding their power resources, then it follows that negotiators with greater skills in changing perceptions have opportunities to increase their side's relative power over the other.

This is not to suggest that there are no limits to what can be achieved through the exercise of negotiation skills or, indeed, through leveraging the other sources of power. In any negotiation the context usually imposes a limit to what can be achieved. The difficulty, of course, for negotiators is that they cannot know in advance what those limits are. Hence the many negotiation behaviours such as bluffing and threatening, that may appear primitive in themselves, but that serve useful purposes in adversarial bargaining. Hence also the fact that many commentators consider negotiation to be more akin to an art than a science!

STRENGTHS OF ADVERSARIAL BARGAINING

We lack research on the role and effectiveness of adversarial bargaining in Irish workplaces. Nevertheless it is possible to suggest some of the main advantages for managers and trade unions of this approach. Firstly, the process is widely understood and accepted by managers and union members and it is seen as the tried and tested method for resolving certain types of disputes, especially disputes over pay, job security and conditions of employment. Therefore, the outcomes have validity (if not always accept-ability) in the eyes of union members and managers. Secondly, the methods that we have described above require little risk taking on the part of negotiators (e.g. they don't risk showing their true positions for fear of being taken advantage of) and this fits well with traditional low trust, 'arms length' management-union relations.

Thirdly, most negotiators have been trained in adversarial tactics by their organisations and trade unions, as well as in the 'school of hard knocks', and they are generally adept in its use. Although it has been argued that over the long run of national programmes since the late 1980s, the bargaining skills of many negotiators have weakened by depriving them of opportunities to practice around the many issues now settled centrally through these programmes, not to mention issues now settled through legislation or the various binding third party mechanisms.

Fourthly, when impasses or breakdowns are reached the state provides effective third party services through the Labour Relations Commission and Labour Court. Finally, at an emotional level, adversarial bargaining is the well-warn path, the familiar and comfortable, to which those who are fearful of changing to an unknown will, and do, cling in resistance.

LIMITATIONS OF ADVERSARIAL BARGAINING

There is some evidence that managers consider adversarial bargaining to be more effective in the handling of pay and conditions than in the handling of issues such as changing the way work is organised and performed, introducing new organisational structures, improving customer service etc (O'Dowd, 2002). There is also evidence that managers prefer to use their own authority in making decisions about organisational change and to involve employees directly in workplace issues than to negotiate with trade unions (Roche and Geary, 1998).

Some commentators have gone so far as to argue that adversarial bargaining no longer provides a viable basis for relations between employees, unions and employers. This argument suggests that adversarial bargaining cannot deliver either on employer concerns for business success or employee/trade union concerns for greater involvement in the types of workplace decision making that is likely to influence job security and conditions of employment (Roche and Gunnigle, 1995; Murphy, 1997).

The main features of adversarial collective bargaining that are considered as limitations are its tendency to encourage low trust relations and its inherent win-lose assumptions. Other reasons cited are the frequent slowness of going through all the procedures, the narrowness of the traditional bargaining agenda and the fact that it does not allow formal input by workers into the formulation of organisation policy and the way work is organised (Roche and Gunnigle, 1995; Turner and Morley, 1995).

We are not aware of any research evidence suggesting what a trade union view on the role and effectiveness of collective bargaining might be. We do know, however, that unions were prominent in seeking the inclusion of clauses on partnership in national programmes from *Partnership 2000* onwards. It seems reasonable, then, to assume that union leaders did not consider it viable to have all the changes likely to take place across the public and private sectors handled through adversarial bargaining. In fact one of the main arguments advanced by trade union leaders in favour of partnership is that it can provide an additional channel of information and influence to members and representatives, particularly in respect to issues not likely to feature on the collective bargaining agenda.

It is clear that unions place a high value on the use of adversarial bargaining. It is precisely through the exercise of such bargaining that trade unions consider their legitimacy to be demonstrated. It is also clear, however, that when their legitimacy is not in question trade unions are open to the use of other forms of problem solving alongside adversarial bargaining (SIPTU, 1999).

It seems reasonable to conclude, then, that many managers and trade union representatives are likely to acknowledge certain limitations of adversarial bargaining and to accept that they need alternative ways of handling issues at workplace level, especially issues around organisational change and improvement. This is largely because of the intensity of change that is happening and due to happen in both the private and public sectors and because the nature of these issues makes them difficult to handle through traditional adversarial bargaining.

PRESSURES FOR CHANGE IN WORKPLACE RELATIONSHIPS

Needless to say, significant changes in how managers and union representatives negotiate and work together does not come about without strong internal and external pressures (Kochan and Dyer, 1976). Effecting significant changes aimed at bringing the parties closer together, carries significant risks for trade unions and managers.

For trade unions there is the risk of members questioning the need for a union, of leaders being 'co-opted' by management and losing touch with members, and of being associated with unpopular decisions. There is the added risk that management will get benefits such as increased work effort with no tangible gains for members in return (Kochan et al, 1984; McKersie, 2002).

The major risk for employers is that closer trade union involvement will either stymie change completely or lead to change on a very slow timetable (McKersie, 2002). Other risks include perceived loss of managerial authority, upset among middle managers and supervisors arising from fear of loss of employment, the high costs of training, and time wasted at meetings (Cooke, 1990).

The National Centre for Partnership and Performance has identified the key pressures currently driving change in both the private and public sectors, including industrial and employee relations structures and practices (NCPP, 2004(b)). See the findings from the private sector in Box 2.1 below.

BOX 2.1: PRESSURES FOR CHANGE IN THE PRIVATE SECTOR

Pressures for Change in the Private Sector		
Competition/Markets	Labour Force	Operating Environment
• Competition from other companies • Competition from subsidiaries • Customer demands • Change in size and nature of markets for goods and services • Product innovation	• Difficulties in recruiting appropriate staff • Employee demands for changes in work place practices • Labour costs and benefits • Labour regulation and legislation	• Changes in production technology • Product and production legislation and regulation • Fluctuations in exchange rates • Insurance costs • Other operating costs

Source: National Centre for Partnership and Performance: The Changing Workplace: A Survey of Employers' Views and Experiences, 2004.

In the private sector the strongest pressures are external and emanate from highly competitive markets in the shape of competition from other companies, from subsidiaries within groups of companies, from customer demands and from market growth and decline and the introduction of new products.

In addition, a number of key aspects of the labour market were identified as important drivers of change. These are difficulties in recruiting appropriate staff, employee demands for changes in workplace practices, labour costs and benefits and labour legislation and regulation. Finally, the operating environment presented challenges in the form of changes in production technology, product innovation, product and production legislation and regulation (e.g. environmental, health and safety), fluctuations in exchange rates, insurance and operating costs.

The most important responses to these pressures were identified as product innovation and marketing. One of the human resource responses to these pressures has been to devise ways of increasing staff involvement in decision making and problem solving (NCPP, 2004(b)).

In the public sector strong internal pressures supplement the external pressures, as outlined in Box 2.2 overleaf. The strongest external pressures emanate from EU and national regulatory changes, from scrutiny from the mass media, requirements for increased effieciency in service delivery, and from the provisions of public service modernisation agendas and national partnership programmes.

Internal pressures include employee demands for better pay and conditions, demands for a greater say and involvement in their work, and demands for better pay. Other internal factors are the introduction of new technology and the requirements of equality and diversity policies.

It is worth noting that this research also indicates that managers in the public services considered the level of willingness to change among staff and trade unions to be a barrier to change. They regarded a lack of flexibility in local industrial relations negotiations as a barrier to change as well (NCPP, 2004(b)).

BOX 2.2: PRESSURES FOR CHANGE IN THE PUBLIC SECTOR

Pressures for Change in the Public Sector		
Internal Pressures	External Pressures	
• Employee needs and preferences for greater flexibility • Demands from staff for greater say and involvement in work • Demands from staff for better pay • Demands from staff for new reward systems, e.g. profit sharing/share options • Introduction of new technology • Explicit equality and diversity policies	1. Regulatory Control • National regulations, legislation, or policy • European/ international regulations • Legislation, e.g. equality in the work place 2. Accountability • Media scrutiny • Freedom of information 3. Service Provision • Requirements for increased efficiency in service delivery	• Requirements for changing opening/closing times to suit clients/users 4. Public Service • Public service modernisation agenda • Budget constraints • Achieving balanced regional development • Adhering to social partnership agreements • Availability of qualified staff.

Source: National Centre for Partnership and Performance: The Changing Workplace: A Survey of Employers' Views and Experiences, 2004

It is against this background of widespread pressures on organisations that the traditional assumptions of adversarial bargaining and 'good industrial relations' have come to be increasingly questioned and found wanting, as seen earlier, not just by management but also, perhaps to a lesser extent, by trade unions. This is also the context in which the many private and public sector partnership initiatives have grown in recent years.

PARTNERSHIP AS A RESPONSE TO THESE PRESSURES

Against a background of generations of low trust, 'arms length' relationships, the introduction of partnership at workplace level constituted a radical innovation. Partnership was not just a new structure: it was a new and different process that created challenges for those taking part but especially for management and union representatives who traditionally engaged with each other through adversarial collective bargaining (O'Dwyer et al, 2002).

On the evidence to date, unionised companies that adopt a partnership approach tend to have an adversarial industrial relations history and climate. With certain exceptions, most have poor management-workforce communications and this is often at the heart of industrial relations problems. Most companies have a strong 'them and us' culture typified by low employee trust in management, low levels of employee involvement in workplace change and considerable employee fear of change and flexibility (Healy, 2002).

In many instances companies have subscribed to change programmes in previous years that have faltered with only temporary successes achieved. Workforce resistance, based on deep-seated mistrust of management, seemed to ensure that the changes had never properly taken root (O'Dowd, 2002).

The adoption of partnership approaches may, therefore, be seen as an implicit acceptance by management and union representatives of the limitations of the adversarial bargaining model. Furthermore, through successive national programmes management and trade unions have explicitly accepted that cooperative as opposed to adversarial working relationships are the key to managing change and higher performance and creating a better workplace. Consequently, these programmes suggest, the handling of a broad range of issues should be amenable to resolution through a partnership approach rather than being permitted to develop into industrial relations difficulties (Government of Ireland, 2003).

What, then, does a 'partnership approach' mean in practice and how is it expected that managers, union representatives and employees will bring issues to resolution and avoid industrial relations difficulties?

PARTNERSHIP PROCESSES

Partnership generally means the establishment of some new structures such as committees or working groups that are considered to be separate from adversarial bargaining and that facilitate managers, employees and union representatives in the discussion and resolution of issues of mutual concern. Partnerships can take many forms including information sharing, consultation, and the sharing of decision making authority (Roche and Turner, 1998). The membership of partnership bodies varies considerably from case to case in terms of the mix of managers, union representatives and individual employees. Partnership bodies are found at the apex or strategic levels of some organisations and at 'shop floor' or operational levels in others. In some cases there are partnership bodies at both levels.

In the unionised sector it is commonly held that partnership bodies should not deal with 'hard' or contentious collective bargaining issues at least during the formative stages and not before the process is robust enough to manage these issues (Government of Ireland, 1997; ICTU, 1997; IBEC, 1998). In most cases the exclusion of collective bargaining issues from the partnership agenda appears to prove helpful in the early stages but as cooperation and trust develop this restriction is frequently weakened by ad hoc agreement between the parties (Roche, 2002). It appears that managers and employees find it hard to maintain an ongoing separation between partnership and adversarial bargaining because issues being handled in one channel affect the other (O'Donnell and Teague, 2000).

Partnership meetings typically work through what might be termed a 'loose' process of open dialogue in which all participants are encouraged to actively participate. Participants commonly adopt ground rules aimed at supporting openness, respect and active listening. Decisions, where they arise, are usually reached through consensus rather than voting. In many cases, but by no means in all, the parties use the services of facilitators to help them establish effective patterns of communication and to avoid conflict along 'them and us' lines.

Partnership bodies may also use more structured methods such as 'joint problem solving' to discuss and resolve issues. The term 'joint problem solving' is used in the main to denote an alternative approach to adversarial bargaining (HSNPF, 2004). Instead of 'across the table' bargaining joint problem solving implies 'around the table' dialogue and consensual decision making with the parties meeting as problem solvers rather than as adversaries (HSNPF, 2004). In some cases partnership groups use formal joint problem solving methodologies such as the 'six steps' problem solving model. This model suggests taking a problem through six steps as follows: defining the problem, gathering information about the problem, suggesting alternative solutions, selecting the best solution, implementing that solution, and reviewing the outcome.

REVIEWS OF PARTNERSHIP

Reviews of partnership in both the private and public sectors indicate that the broad experience has been positive for management, unions and employees. A review of formal partnership arrangements in the civil service, for example, concluded that managers and employees welcomed the opportunity that partnership afforded them to engage in a non-confrontational forum, notwithstanding the uneven development of partnership across that system (O'Dwyer et al, 2002).

There is also growing evidence of positive performance outcomes relating to costs, competitiveness, production processes, product quality, effort to get the job done, as well as improved workforce productivity and business performance (Totterdill and Sharpe, 1999; NCPP, 2002; O'Dowd, 2002). There is also some evidence of positive relationships outcomes such as greater employee understanding of customer needs, improved communications and trust, a better appreciation of how to manage change, reduced conflict, better mutual understanding between management and trade unions, more effective use of collective bargaining, and a reduced use of third parties to resolve disputes (Healy, 2000; NCPP, 2002).

Positive outcomes for employees that have been identified include: greater confidence and self-esteem, greater insights into business problems, more control over work leading to increased job satisfaction, a say in workplace organisation and some influence over business decisions, influence over strategic business decisions, more time for family life arising from annualised hours and elimination of overtime, employee share ownership, and a better quality of working life (Totterdill and Sharpe, 1999; NCPP, 2002; Hastings, 2003). There is also some evidence of stabilised industrial relations and improved organisational performance leading to better security of employment as well as enhanced terms and conditions (NCPP, 2002).

Overall, partnership appears to have helped to develop relationships, to improve communications and to build trust between management and trade unions. Where changes were introduced through partnership they were said to 'stick' (O'Dwyer et al, 2002).

Partnership, therefore, appears to provide important opportunities for management and trade unions to open up, explore and resolve issues in what is often called a 'safe space' of a kind that is not available within traditional collective bargaining based as it is on firmly established positions and counter positions.

PARTNERSHIP WEAKNESSES

Many management and trade union representatives have commented, on the other hand, that the partnership process can be very slow and that the agenda so far has been limited to 'soft' issues such as human resource practices and the quality of the working environment (Roche, 2002). In many instances, partnership bodies have encountered problems dealing with difficult or contentious issues such as the types of issues normally handled through adversarial bargaining. This is not surprising given how deeply embedded adversarial collective bargaining is in most unionised organisations. Indeed, such difficulties appear to be common to partnerships in both the private and public sectors internationally (Roche, 2002).

Problems around partnership and adversarial bargaining can arise for a number of reasons. In some cases familiarity and comfort with the traditional way of doing business can militate against new approaches based on open dialogue and consensus (O'Dwyer et al, 2002). In other cases, management and trade unions may hold diverging views as to how partnership and adversarial bargaining should be aligned and may not have ways of resolving these differences.

In some cases there is insufficient training and inadequate usage of joint problem solving (O'Dwyer et al, 2002). In yet other cases the parties simply find that the open dialogue process is not sufficiently 'robust' to handle issues around which parties have strongly conflicting viewpoints. In the local government and health sectors, for example, reviews of partnership suggest that trade union officials and managers have concerns as to whether the partnership process is robust enough for the handling of significant change issues (Roche, 2002). In some cases the very existence of the open dialogue process leads to conflict which participants are unprepared for and do not know how to handle effectively. This can be particularly acute where the parties have no skilled facilitators to help them work their way out of conflicts.

Others have found that it is not possible to bring every issue to finality through partnership. In such cases issues have to be transferred into the adversarial bargaining system and perhaps ultimately on to the Labour Relations Commission.

INTEREST-BASED BARGAINING AS A ROBUST PROCESS

Interest-based bargaining has, in our view, strong potential for helping parties to handle the difficulties outlined above and to expand and deepen their partnerships. Like adversarial bargaining, interest-based bargaining is a form of collective bargaining that requires the involvement of management and union negotiators whether the latter are full-time negotiators or local elected representatives. In this sense interest-based bargaining assumes the legitimate and necessary involvement of trade unions in the handling of agreed upon issues. It makes explicit, rather than hides, the fact that there can be significantly different interests between management and trade unions as far as certain issues are concerned.

As a process, interest-based bargaining is designed to be used on a very wide range of issues including major changes and distributive issues relating to pay and conditions of employment. Interest-based bargaining has a robust set of procedures and techniques. At the same time interest-based bargaining is based on assumptions of mutual gains and uses procedures that are designed to generate high quality solutions while also enhancing relationships.

In this sense it may, for certain organisations, be a 'breakthrough strategy' that will facilitate the movement forward of the partnership agenda from so-called 'soft' issues to 'hard' or contentious issues. The local government and health sectors in Ireland provide two examples where management and trade unions are seeking to use interest-based bargaining or problem solving as a means of deepening the partnership agenda and strengthening the partnership process.

INTEREST-BASED BARGAINING IN LOCAL GOVERNMENT

In local government it has become clear to senior managers and union representatives that they can achieve more through partnership than they are currently achieving. They have concluded that the extent to which significant benefits will come from partnership will depend on the extent to which they are prepared to put significant issues into the partnership process (LANPAG, 2003).

For that reason, they have recently agreed on procedures for handling significant changes through partnership in a document titled *Handling Significant Changes through Partnership* (LANPAG, 2005), as outlined in Box 2.3 overleaf.

The document specifically recommends the use of interest-based problem solving as a key tool in the partnership process. The aim of these procedures is to help managers, trade union representatives and employees working through partnership to handle significant changes with confidence. *Handling Significant Changes through Partnership* lists the types of issues that managers and trade union representatives have identified as being important to address through partnership in the interests of improving services to the public and the quality of working life of managers and employees.

BOX 2.3: INTEREST-BASED PROBLEM SOLVING IN LOCAL GOVERNMENT

Handling Significant Changes Through Partnership

The partnership process provides a neutral ground on which managers can meet staff and their representatives to tease out their various perspectives on the issues facing each and on the opportunities and constraints in changing or improving how things are done. Where there is agreement between management and unions, many issues can be decided and implemented through partnership and in cases where there is no agreement, much progress can be made through partnership to ensure that differences are resolved in ways which retain the confidence, trust and morale of all staff in the way conflict or differences are managed.

Where there is agreement to have certain matters decided or implemented through partnership the problem-solving aspect of partnership is being seen as one of its main strengths. In this context it will be important for local management and union representatives to be familiar with the two main problem-solving approaches and to become adept in their use:

- Joint problem solving when there is broad agreement around the necessity for a particular change and where the parties want to work together to find the best solution
- Interest-based problem solving when there is broad agreement around the necessity for a particular change but different interests among management and staff that need to be factored into the pursuit of a best solution.

Source: Local Authority National Partnership Advisory Group: Handling Significant Changes through Partnership, 2005.

The document sets out a framework within which managers and union representatives may raise significant issues and agree on appropriate mechanisms for handling them. The document also sets out a number of supports that may be called on by the parties in the event that difficulties arise. At the time of writing the Local Authority National Partnership Advisory Group is sponsoring a number of pilot projects aimed at helping the management and trade unions in local authorities to implement the new arrangements.

INTEREST-BASED BARGAINING IN THE HEALTH SECTOR

In the health sector, the Department of Health and Children and the health service management and trade unions have agreed an 'action plan for people management' (DOHC, 2002). This plan addresses the training and development needs of managers, employees and union representatives.

The plan is presented as an aid to the 'mainstreaming' of partnership, i.e. the development of a culture in which joint problem solving and joint decision making become the norm. It proposes the development of interest-based bargaining/problem solving through local partnership structures.

The Health Services National Partnership Forum (HSNPF) has published a guide to the use of what they call 'tools for change through partnership' (HSNPF, 2004), see Box 2.4 below. These are described as a range of change techniques that sit comfortably with the partnership process.

BOX 2.4: INTEREST-BASED BARGAINING IN THE HEALTH SECTOR

HSNPF: Tools for Change	

• Getting to Yes
• Interest-Based Bargaining
• Interest-Based
  Problem Solving/
  Joint Problem Solving
• Alternative Dispute Resolution
• Integrated Conflict
  Management Systems
	• Conflict Resolution
	• Mediation
	• Facilitation
	• Future Search Conference
	• Open Space Technology
	• Hamburger Model
	• Edward de Bono's Six Thinking Hats

Source: Health Services National Partnership Forum: Tools for Change Through Partnership, 2004.

There has been a significant degree of interest among managers and union representatives in the tools for change and a number of workshops and training courses have been held around them.

Interest-based bargaining (the model described in the HSPNPF document is the one used by the Federal Mediation and Conciliation Service in the U.S. and described in this book) is presented as one of the principles of the partnership process. Based on consensus decision making it gives everyone around the table a voice. As the expertise and experience of all the parties is shared it should lead to higher quality decisions that have a greater chance of being implemented because all those around the table will have shared responsibility for the result.

CHAPTER SUMMARY

In this chapter we saw that the adversarial bargaining model operated around assumptions of a low trust, 'arms length' relationship between management and trade unions. The types of behaviours used in adversarial bargaining made sense within these assumptions. Market and other pressures were, however, casting doubt on the continuing usefulness to both management and trade unions of a bargaining model that kept the parties at 'arms length' when, arguably, they needed to work more closely together to ensure the viability of organisations and the jobs and conditions of employment of those working in them.

In many organisations management and trade unions have adopted what they term 'partnership' ways of working together. In general, these partnership initiatives have worked well for the parties concerned, not least in giving them a process through which they can talk more openly about issues of mutual concern than they can in the adversarial framework. Difficulties have commonly arisen within partnership bodies when they have tried to tackle difficult or contentious issues. Interest-based bargaining offers a robust process that can help the parties to address such issues while continuing to develop cooperative relationships. We now turn to a more detailed discussion of interest-based bargaining in Chapter 3.

-3-

INTEREST-BASED BARGAINING

'The single most important difference between the new interest-based bargaining and traditional collective bargaining is that issues are brought to the table rather than positions. We discuss the issue without any pre-planned proposal for solutions. Another big difference, and a very welcome change, is that the interest-based approach requires you to be at the table together, interacting nose to nose. There are no long periods of separation'.
Management Negotiating Team Member.

'I have been a union representative for the past fourteen years.   Having worked on four contracts I must admit that in the beginning I was sceptical. Now that we have been through it, all I can say is 'why did it take us so long to get to this point?' It was a very comfortable exchange of ideas. I am used to having my stomach in knots but there was none of that'
Union Negotiating Team Member.

INTRODUCTION

IN THIS CHAPTER we give an overview of the main features of an interest-based approach to collective bargaining and we introduce the PAST Model of IBB that the US author of the book developed for use in US workplaces. We contrast this with the adversarial bargaining approach that has commonly been used in Irish organizations. We discuss reasons why it can make sense to use the interest-based approach and we highlight a number of situations where it might usefully be adopted. Finally, we outline the main benefits that are accredited to interest-based bargaining.

INTEREST-BASED BARGAINING

Interest-based bargaining or IBB has several different names. It has been called 'integrative bargaining', 'win-win bargaining', 'principled negotiations', 'getting to yes' and 'mutual gains bargaining' among others. We have already described interest-based bargaining as an approach to collective bargaining that is focused on understanding and building on interests, and using problem solving tools as a way of avoiding positional conflicts, and achieving better outcomes for all stakeholders. It uses a range of skills and tools such as active listening, converting positions into underlying needs or interests, joint data collection, brainstorming, joint task forces, facilitation, and effective communication with constituents (Fonstad et al, 2004).

Two books provide the source of most of the ideas associated with interest-based bargaining. These are Walton and McKersie's *Behavioural Theory of Labour Negotiations* (Walton and McKersie, 1965) and Fisher and Ury's *Getting to Yes: Negotiating Agreements Without Giving In* (Fisher and Ury, 1983).

Interest-based bargaining is possible when the nature of a problem allows for solutions which benefit both parties or when the gains of one party do not represent equal sacrifices by the other. Interest-based bargaining is particularly suitable for handling issues such as organisational improvement and change where there is potential scope for gains by both sides. The terms 'interest-based bargaining' and 'IBB' are used throughout this text because they seems to the authors to capture the essential difference between this form of bargaining or problem solving and traditional adversarial bargaining which is the emphasis on surfacing and addressing interests as opposed to bargaining around positions.

Interest-based approaches to resolving disputes can be contrasted with the two other significant ways of resolving conflicts. These are power and rights based approaches (Ury et al, 1988).

POWER, RIGHTS, INTERESTS

A dispute starts when one party or organisation makes a claim or demand on another who rejects it. In any dispute, people have certain interests at stake. They have certain standards or rights against which they can consider what a reasonable outcome to their dispute might be. And there is a certain balance of power between the parties to the dispute. Interests, rights and power are, then, three basic elements of any dispute (Ury et al, 1988). In seeking to resolve a dispute the parties can seek to resolve that dispute by focusing on one or more of these elements.

Interests are the needs, desires, and concerns that underlie the positions that people adopt in disputes or negotiations. They are the things that people care about. Reconciling different interests is not always easy and may in some cases be extremely difficult.

Rights are independent standards such as precedent, seniority, fairness etc that may be fixed through legislation or through collective agreements or through 'custom and practice'. But rights are not always clear and disputes around rights might end up before third parties for resolution or even before the courts.

Power is the capacity that one party has at any given time to force its position on a particular issue on another party. Exercising power usually means imposing costs on the other party, e.g. when employers enforce changes or when unions take industrial action. Power-based approaches to resolving disputes tend to be of two types. One is power-based negotiation of the adversarial type where parties threaten each other. The other is when one or both parties actually take action to determine who will win, e.g. employers enforce changes or unions take industrial action.

There is a relationship between interests, rights and power that needs to be considered. A party may wish to use an interest-based approach to solving a dispute but the other party may not. If the other party has much greater power then it is not likely that they will be persuaded to take an interest-based approach. A party may solve a dispute on the basis of a third party confirming their rights. But if they do not have the power to enforce that decision then the dispute will continue.

No single way of handling conflicts can be judged superior to others in all cases. Ways of handling conflicts can be judged in terms of effectiveness using three main considerations:

- Costs: how much time, money, and emotional energy is expended in resolving the conflict?
- Satisfaction with outcomes: how satisfied are the parties with the outcome?
- Effect on relationships: what is the effect of the way the conflict was resolved on relationships over the long term?

Power approaches are considered to be the most costly approaches not just in terms of costs to those directly involved but also to third parties affected by disputes such as company suppliers and customers or members of the public (Ury et al, 1988). Days can be lost due to various forms of industrial action, sickness and absenteeism rates can be high and management-employee relations can become strained if not embittered. Trust and cooperation at work are key intangible assets for the advancement of competitiveness, but they are also the first casualties when grievances are allowed to develop without resolution (LRC, 2005).

Rights approaches are considered next most costly while interest-based approaches are considered least costly to those concerned (Ury et al, 1988). It has already been noted in Chaper 1 the extent to which various conditions of employment are now established as rights by legislation in Ireland compared to ten years ago.

STRATEGIC NEGOTIATIONS

In the language of 'strategic negotiations', interest-based bargaining is a 'fostering' approach towards the introduction of changes affecting employees and trade unions, i.e. one designed to effect change by developing high commitment among employees and a more cooperative relationship between management and the union. Fostering is seen as a modification of the traditional 'arms length' relationship that frequently leads to some form of partnership (Walton et al, 1994).

Fostering is contrasted with two other approaches available to management and trade unions. These are 'forcing' (a power-based strategy) where management responds to the need for change by attempting to force economic concessions and changes in work arrangements by unilateral action and by bargaining power, and 'escape' which involves management either closing unionised operations and moving to a non-union environment or developing policies and practices aimed at keeping an operation non-union.

These strategies are not mutually exclusive. In the context of major change initiatives in Irish semi-state companies, for example, it emerged that there were patterns of forcing and fostering, either operating sequentially or in parallel, depending on the nature of industrial relations in the company (Hastings, 2003).

POWER AND INTEREST-BASED BARGAINING

We have already seen that power is at the heart of the adversarial bargaining process and that it is a critical element in influencing outcomes. Why, then, would parties agree not to have recourse to power as the basis for reaching a settlement as they are expected to do in an interest-based approach? Advocates of interest-based bargaining are not so naive as to believe that power will disappear and an egalitarian environment will emerge simply because the parties agree to engage in IBB and use standards.

Logically, it would seem that the only sound reason for not relying on power is that the parties are convinced that they can achieve outcomes of greater value to them, and at an acceptable cost, by not relying on power, i.e. by cooperating to make the organization work better for both management and employee stakeholders rather than fighting over what is currently available (Cooke, 1990). The types of outcomes that are valued by management, employees and unions include both extrinsic rewards such as higher wages and higher profits and intrinsic rewards such as job satisfaction, recognition for work well done, employee openness to change, employee commitment to organizational goals etc (Cooke, 1990).

Discretionary effort is something that is sought by managers as a means of enhancing performance and productivity. Where management and trade unions are cooperating to improve organisational performance such discretionary effort is likely to be increased. Employees who feel a genuine sense of involvement in and ownership of decisions affecting their work and the results of their work commonly extend themselves through additional discretionary effort that benefits themselves and the organisation. This is an example of achieving more through cooperation than through power.

Another example is when management and trade unions agree to handle certain issues through partnership rather than through adversarial bargaining. They are, in effect, making a decision to forego the use of power against each other. Management, for example, may be foregoing the right to unilaterally decide a change issue on the assumption that they can achieve consensus around it in which case the commitment of employees and trade unions will be a powerful asset in implementing the change.

Similarly a trade union might forego pursuing a claim through adversarial bargaining on the assumption that they can achieve a consensus on it and forego having to use the formal industrial relations procedures. Or, indeed, where parties are working to improve relationships they may consider a non-adversarial approach to be of benefit in itself in that it helps to improve relationships and helps to create a climate in which parties are more likely to behave in a cooperative way towards each other.

Ultimately, what the IBB approach asks of the parties is to agree that, for the purposes of these negotiations, they will not resort to power. Instead they will develop and use standards to determine what they will agree upon. Interest-based bargaining does not eliminate power, only the resort to power.

THE PAST MODEL

Box 3.1 summarises the principles, assumptions, steps and techniques used in the interest-based bargaining model being described in this book (Barrett, 1996). While this model was developed for use in management-union negotiations it can, and has been, used in other types of disputes such as community or neighbourhood disputes, civil rights disputes, environmental disputes, to mention only some.

The principles are well established within the field of conflict resolution at this stage (Blake et al, 1964; Walton and McKersie, 1965; Fisher and Ury, 1983). They suggest focusing on issues or problems and not on personalities or people but instead spending time at the outset on defining the problem rather than going straight into the exchange of proposals and counter proposals, as happens in adversarial bargaining.

The principles suggest going beneath surface issues to get at underlying interests, fears and concerns. They advise trying to ensure that each party comes out a winner by generating a range of solutions that can be judged and agreed by some objective standards rather than by power. This last is really important. If problem solving is to lead to effective and mutually satisfactory solutions then the parties need to substitute some measure of objectivity for assessing solutions rather than loyalty to their side or simply 'winning' (Blake et al, 1964).

The assumptions are perhaps the most important elements in that without these assumptions the steps and techniques would not be used at all. Key assumptions are that mutual gain is possible, that bargaining can be conducted in a manner that enhances rather than damages relationships, and that reliance on power can be avoided if certain steps are followed.

These assumptions are markedly different from the assumptions that underpin adversarial bargaining. As seen earlier, the adversarial industrial relations tradition assumes a pervasive conflict of interest between management and trade unions and a low trust, power-based approach to dispute resolution.

BOX 3.1 PAST MODEL OF INTEREST-BASED BARGAINING

Principles	• Focus on issues not on personalities • Focus on interests not on positions • Seek mutual gain • Use a fair method to determine outcomes
Assumptions	• Bargaining enhances the parties' relationship • Both parties can win in bargaining • Parties should help each other to win • Open and frank discussion and information sharing expands the areas of mutual interests and this in turn expands the options available to the parties • Mutually developing standards for evaluating options can move decision making away from reliance on power
Steps	Pre-Bargaining Steps: • Prepare for bargaining • Develop opening statements Bargaining Steps • Agree on a list of issues and focus on one at a time • Identify interests on one issue • Develop options on one issue • Create acceptable standards • Test options with standards to achieve solution or settlement
Techniques	• Idea charting • Brainstorming • Consensus decision making

For IBB to work effectively some advance planning and preparation is needed. The parties appoint bargaining teams, take joint training, agree their agenda, agree on how they will organise the bargaining or problem solving sessions, decide what their information needs are around the agenda items, and make other arrangements such as choosing a facilitator.

The steps follow closely on standard problem solving steps. First, the parties select an issue they both want to resolve. Then they identify their interests around that issue, initially in separate sessions and then in a joint session. Next they generate options to satisfy those interests using brainstorming and flipcharting. Finally, they agree on objective criteria for evaluating the different options before selecting their preferred ones.

The key techniques are idea charting, brainstorming and consensus decision making. These are not generally used in adversarial bargaining. However, as we saw earlier, such techniques and others are becoming increasingly familiar to managers, employees and union representatives who are involved in different forms of joint working such as partnership or teams or various forms of problem solving and improvement processes in the workplace. In Chapter 6 we describe these techniques in greater detail .

ADVERSARIAL AND INTEREST-BASED APPROACHES COMPARED

It will be clear from the discussion above that there are significant differences between traditional adversarial and interest-based approaches to workplace bargaining. These differences are summarized in Box 3.2 below.

In adversarial bargaining the main focus is for each party to win as much as possible while giving up as little as possible. The main focus of IBB, on the other hand, is to ensure that each side comes out satisfied that its interests have been addressed such that both sides can win.

In adversarial bargaining each side looks out for itself. In IBB the sides look out for themselves as well as for each other because the success of one side depends on the success of the other. This is the opposite of the 'win-lose' approach of adversarial bargaining.

At preparation stage there are significant differences too. Adversarial bargainers prepare their positions separately and privately. In IBB the parties work together during preparation by agreeing on the agenda, ground rules and the processes to be used.

BOX 3.2 MAIN FEATURES OF TWO APPROACHES

Adversarial Bargaining	Interest-Based Bargaining
The main focus is to give as little and to get as much as possible	The main focus is to ensure that the interests of each side are addressed
The parties prepare separately by drafting opening positions as targets.	The parties prepare together by agreeing ground rules and ways of working
These positions take the form of 'wish lists'. The parties frequently table 'unreal' positions that they can subsequently 'concede'	The parties prepare separately by discussing interests with constituents. If constituents present positions the negotiators convert these into interests.
They also prepare resistance points above or below which they are not prepared to go.	They approach bargaining with open minds as to what the final agreement might be.
The negotiations take the form of two sides bargaining across a table with breaks for caucus meetings; options are explored in private sessions	The negotiations take the form of one group with occasional breaks for caucus or side meetings; options are openly explored in joint sessions
If the parties undergo negotiation training it is done separately	If using IBB for the first time the parties undergo joint training
The negotiations open with positional statements and follow a sequence of offers and counteroffers with frequent deferrals and breakdowns	The negotiations open with discussions around an issue and each party's interests underlying that issue followed by a problem solving sequence.
Information is kept 'tight' and only disclosed under pressure or to extract a concession.	Information is openly shared and research is usually conducted jointly
Decisions are made by compromise or under pressure.	Decisions are made by consensus after an agreed objective evaluation of options.
Mainly involves industrial relations managers and union officials.	Involvement is extended to others with expertise around relevant topics.
Spokespersons present key positions and moves	Spokespersons outline key interests but all members participate
Each side attempts to keep the other under pressure by power tactics.	The parties agree not to use pressure as a negotiation lever
The parties use a facilitator when they reach an impasse.	The parties use a facilitator during the entire process.

Also, in IBB the parties prepare interests rather than positions and then communicate these interests openly and make them subject to questioning and probing for greater understanding. In IBB the parties undergo joint training as part of the preparation for bargaining. In adversarial bargaining they train separately, if at all.

IBB takes the form of two bargaining teams working together for most of the time but with some separate or caucus meetings. Meetings are more like workshops or problem solving sessions than traditional bargaining sessions. Adversarial bargaining is very much 'them and us' across the table with considerable periods of time spent in separate caucus meetings. The sequence in adversarial bargaining is one of offer and counter-offer whereas IBB follows a joint problem solving sequence that is transparent and logical.

In IBB possible options for settlement are discussed openly in a joint session. In adversarial bargaining this happens behind the scenes between the lead negotiators.

Information is held closely in adversarial bargaining. It is openly disclosed in IBB as a means of helping the problem solving process and of helping to build an open, trusting relationship. From the preparation stage onwards the parties are likely to generate a lot of information together and to analyze that information together rather than having to 'squeeze blood out of a stone' as frequently happens with information in adversarial bargaining.

In IBB, all participants are expected to contribute whereas in adversarial bargaining lead spokespersons 'make the running' most of the time with other participants having support roles. Also, the IBB bargaining or problem solving teams are likely to include individual employees and line managers with expertise rather than just full-time union officials, shop stewards and IR/HR executives.

In adversarial bargaining power tactics such as bluffing and threatening are used in the bargaining sessions and pressure is also generated outside as a means of strengthening hands at the bargaining table. In IBB the parties agree not to use power tactics but to seek agreed methods or criteria for making consensus decisions about final outcomes.

Finally, third parties are usually only used in adversarial bargaining when a breakdown has happened or is imminent whereas bargaining teams using IBB may have external or internal facilitators from the outset to help them to design and manage the process.

CHOOSING INTEREST-BASED BARGAINING

Choosing IBB as a negotiating strategy represents a significant decision and, indeed, risk on the parts of management and trade unions as well as the constituencies that they represent. Not only does IBB involve learning new approaches and skills but, more significantly, as seen above, it involves the parties agreeing not to use power against each other as a means of getting as much for their own side as they can from the bargaining process.

Experience to date shows that the managements and trade unions most likely to adopt IBB in Ireland are those who have already been trying to work together more closely, through some form of workplace partnership, and who have a range of issues that they need to address jointly and that lend themselves to a win-win approach. In such cases IBB is seen as an additional tool in the problem solving toolbox.

Interest-based bargaining is not likely to be effective where there are very high levels of suspicion and mistrust between negotiating teams or where there is only weak support from senior management and trade union leaders. In such cases a period of relationships building may be needed.

Negotiating teams that are strongly focused on short-term gains and are not concerned about relationships in the longer term are not likely to be interested in IBB either.

It is not likely that IBB will be of more than theoretical interest to managements and trade unions who prefer to retain an adversarial 'arms length' relationship and who reckon 'if it ain't broke don't fix it'. Nor is it likely to be of much interest to those who might like to move towards more cooperative working but who are fatalistic about the possibility of achieving a better relationship that can last and that can deliver benefits to both sides at the same time.

If the negotiating parties are not prepared to invest in time, resources and training or if they do not have the resources to do this, then IBB is not likely to work effectively. Or, if the parties are looking for quick and easy solutions then IBB won't provide that since it takes training, time, effort and determination.

When thinking about whether to use a cooperative approach to bargaining or problem solving such as IBB, or a more competitive approach such as adversarial bargaining, it makes sense to consider three main factors in the situation. These are the issues that the parties want to address, the parties who will be directly involved in the process, and the context or circumstances in which they are currently operating, as illustrated in Diagram 3.1 below (Ware, 1980).

DIAGRAM 3.1 CHOOSING A BARGAINING STRATEGY

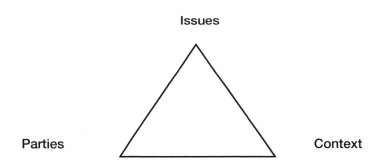

Choosing a negotiation strategy is not easy and two parties may well have different views as to how they want to conduct their bargaining. In addition, every negotiation situation has distinctive characteristics. Nevertheless, this framework should prove useful in thinking about the factors that need to be taken into account regardless of what the situation might be.

ISSUES

Probably the most important factor and the one that the parties are likely to consider first is the nature of the issues to be addressed. As suggested earlier, while IBB can in theory be used to negotiate any issue, some issues are more likely to lend themselves to this approach than others. If there is one issue only and it is primarily distributive, i.e. involving scarce resources then adversarial bargaining is likely to be the first approach to be considered.

If, on the other hand, the issues are unresolved technical or procedural problems, i.e. how to do something differently such that the solution may benefit all the parties then IBB may be a more effective way of addressing the issues. Problems that are complex and that do not have obvious solutions require some collaboration, for example the sharing of knowledge and expertise.

If the problems are complex and uncertain and without obvious solutions, as many problems to do with organisational change and improvement are, then a problem solving approach is more likely to be effective. Again, the sharing of knowledge and expertise that takes place in IBB can help in the search for a solution that works well and that is acceptable to both sides.

Management-union negotiations invariably involve a number of issues rather than a single one. This can help the parties to reach agreement, as each of them may be able to afford to 'gain on the swings and lose on the roundabouts', This is also true of interest-based negotiations.

Another important question is how important is the issue to each of the parties and to the parties together? Interest-based bargaining can be a demanding and time consuming process. If the parties are not equally concerned to find a solution then the willingness to give the time and effort needed to make the process work may not be forthcoming.

PARTIES AND THEIR RELATIONSHIPS

The quality of relationships between the parties directly involved in the bargaining or problem solving and their constituents will also influence the decision about which approach to use. IBB is more likely to work well when the parties feel free to share openly their knowledge, ideas and concerns. An open, trusting relationship facilitates this sharing. Trust can build up during the problem solving process but if trust levels are very low to start off with then the parties may be more likely to opt for adversarial bargaining.

On the other hand, if having better relationships over the long term is an important goal for both parties then they may find it important to invest the time and effort in developing that relationship through the bargaining process as well as outside it.

If the parties do not understand and accept each other it is more likely that they will opt for adversarial bargaining since this doesn't require the same degree of openness or information sharing. Cooperative problem solving requires a degree of risk-taking and experimentation that benefits from sound relationships.

Another important question to ask is whether the parties have the authority to make changes relating to the issues or problems concerned. If either party is severely constrained in making decisions about outcomes then there are likely to be frequent interruptions by the need to clear what is happening with others who are not directly involved. Such interruptions tend to be time consuming and may decrease the level of trust and respect between the parties.

Another important aspect of the relationship between the parties is the power dimension. Interest-based bargaining is unlikely to happen where one party has considerably more power than the other. The party with more power is likely to be less interested in expending the time and energy needed for this approach. The less powerful side is also likely to be reluctant to be open about their interests and concerns as they may consider the other side will see this as a sign of weakness.

Personal values and preferences also come into play. Not all negotiators will have confidence either in the interest-based process itself or perhaps in themselves to use it effectively. There may be situations where a management or union negotiator may have to stand aside to let someone else take a leading role at least until they have become more confident in the process and in themselves. There will, as seen earlier, always be some negotiators who have become so institutionalised in adversarial thinking and behaviours that they consider this way of bargaining to be part of 'human nature' and, therefore, not capable of being changed.

CONTEXT

Then there is the issue of context. In some contexts there is active encouragement for the use of IBB. In the case of local authorities and health agencies in Ireland, for example, there are national policies and agreements that encourage the use of interest-based approaches. If, on the other hand, the management and union groups represented in the negotiations expect their representatives to negotiate in an adversarial manner then it will be difficult for these representatives to do otherwise and to continue to enjoy the support and confidence of their constituencies.

If agreements have to be reached very quickly then IBB may not be suited to the situation. Apart from time, other important resources that will be needed include monies for training, data collection, facilitation etc.

SITUATIONS IN WHICH IBB MIGHT HELP

Workshop participants (management and union negotiators and facilitators) in Ireland suggested a number of situations in which interest-based bargaining could be helpful to management and trade unions. These were:

- Where organisations already have joint management-union groups, are using some joint problem solving approaches and want to extend their joint working into more traditional bargaining agendas and into major change issues, adopting an interest-based approach could help
- Where the parties want to have a more cooperative relationship but are reluctant to have formal structures, interest-based bargaining might be effective in improving relationships without having to have permanent structures in place
- In the introduction of modernisation programmes in government departments, interest-based bargaining could empower local union and staff representatives by providing a structure and effective tools and techniques through which they could engage in a meaningful way with the management agenda
- Where management and unions recognise the need to change but are fearful of 'losing out' in the change process, interest-based bargaining might provide a methodology to protect their core interests and to reach effective agreements
- Where there has been a recent negative bargaining experience or where relationships are very poor, management and trade unions might decide to find a better way to negotiate and may decide to experiment with interest-based bargaining
- Where partnerships have failed, interest-based bargaining could be used as an untainted process that was 'within the spirit of partnership'
- Where organisations are developing information and consultation mechanisms in line with EU Directives, interest-based bargaining could provide a methodology that would avoid adversarial approaches

- Where parties wish to avoid continuously finalising their negotiations on terms proposed by third parties they could use interest-based bargaining as a means of ensuring ownership of settlements
- Where traditional bargaining works well around industrial relations issues but not around organisational change issues, the parties could experiment with interest-based bargaining on some selected issues around organisational change
- Where there is a willingness to try out new approaches, interest-based bargaining could be used by local managers and union representatives to solve individual grievances.

THE EIRCOM CASE

Management and trade unions in Eircom have made extensive use of what they term 'interest based problem solving'. Initially in response to the liberalisation of the telecommunications market and more recently in response to ongoing competitive threats, the management and unions in Eircom agreed to take a 'partnership approach' to organisational change and improvement. This approach included a radical recasting of traditional adversarial bargaining into a new form of joint problem solving (Hastings, 2003).

The objectives of the Eircom partnership are:
- To enhance the prosperity and success of the enterprise
- To create the basis and arrangements for discussion of major decisions affecting the organisation's future, including future economic security
- To engage all stakeholders' ideas, abilities and commitment, and
- To enhance the quality of the working environment.

The principles upon which this partnership was constructed are essentially interest-based and seek to steer the parties away from adversarial assumptions and tactics. They are:
- A shared understanding of the transformation required for the company to be successful
- A recognition that the problems of both parties must be addressed
- That neither side will approach negotiations with the objective of making short-term gains at the expense of the other
- That the focus of the discussions will be to build a business consensus capable of being sustained in the long-term against whatever vicissitudes will inevitably assail it from time to time

- A common ownership of and a willingness to solve problems
- Adoption of a new process to enable key changes to be implemented rapidly to meet business needs.

These principles are enshrined in a form of interest-based problem solving that is used by partnership groups and that takes place as close as possible to where problems arise. Typical agenda items include new working practices, processes and organisation structures aimed at improving workflows and reducing costs. These types of issues would in the past have been handled through adversarial bargaining of a 'pay for change' type in which the union would either agree to a change subject to payment or, more commonly, object to a change and block it until some form of payment had been negotiated.

It is not possible to do justice to the many complex issues that have been resolved using interest-based problem solving in Eircom. Box 3.3 gives an outline of the process used.

Management are obliged to involve the union at the earliest stage in the development of a change and to produce a 'staff impact assessment' at the earliest time during development. The purpose of 'early involvement' is to anticipate and minimise difficulties in implementing changes affecting staff.

Efforts to resolve any staff impact issues must proceed in parallel with the planning and implementation of the changes concerned. Needless to say, a key objective of this approach has been to speed up the pace of change in a context where competitors, most of whom are unburdened with traditional industrial relations arrangements, are actively eating into the company's markets.

In some cases the problem solving groups comprise of local managers, employees and local union representatives and in other cases these are joined by full-time union officials.

Perhaps one of the most interesting aspects of the Eircom system is that the decisions reached by the problem solving teams are not subject to ratification by union committees or by membership ballots as happened in the adversarial system. For this reason, considerable effort is put into consulting and informing those employees who are going to be affected by the outcomes during the course of the problem solving process itself.

BOX 3.3 INTEREST-BASED PROBLEM SOLVING PROCESS IN EIRCOM

Interest-based problem solving in Eircom is described as a next step in the evolution of labour-management relations that honours the collective bargaining process by encouraging parties to get the most out of it. Rather than settling for a war of positions, demands and posturing, this process uses the knowledge, skill and experiences of the parties and, ideally, their organisations, to fully explore the basic interests that are behind the more classic behaviour seen in traditional problem solving. By striving to understand each other's interests, parties build a base of information that not only helps them negotiate a solution that meets these interests but also provides a place from which to continue mutually beneficial endeavours. In the context of partnership and local teams this approach can help further and strengthen the partnership by enabling the parties to develop solutions that are mutually beneficial.

The process uses the following steps:

Know and Understand the Problem:
- Understand the common interests of the parties by identifying and exploring the interests that each party identifies and explains
- Clarify all necessary facts: the known, unknown and to be known facts
- From the common interests and the information generated develop a joint statement of the issue or problem to be addressed

Discover Creative Solutions
- Brainstorm options to satisfy the interests in a process called 'non-binding idea generation'
- Identify potential solutions through discussion of the options and by rating them objectively against standards

Reach Interest Based Agreement
- Reach agreement using consensus decision making
- Evaluate the negotiations

Source: Telecom Eireann/Trade Union Alliance: District and Local Partnership Training, Boyle and Associates (1998).

POTENTIAL BENEFITS

What are the potential benefits to trade unions and management in using interest-based bargaining? The main 'generic' advantages that are advanced by advocates (Barrett, 1996 and 1998; Weiss, 1996; Brommer et al, 2002) on behalf of interest-based bargaining are that

- It can lead to better solutions because all of the necessary information has been made available and a greater number of options arise for consideration
- It helps to create a better ongoing relationship between the negotiating parties by having them work together rather than separately
- It increases respect and trust between the parties because they can see that there are no 'hidden agendas' but rather openly declared mutual and conflicting interests
- It can improve relationships between the wider constituencies as they can see that this is a process based on openness and mutual respect
- It can draw upon existing problem solving skills and help to develop new skills where these do not already exist
- It uses conflict as a means of generating energy and creativity in an environment that is 'safe' for the practitioners because they have prepared new ground rules for this form of bargaining
- The resulting agreements are more durable because they meet the underlying interests and needs of the parties and not just their short term positions
- It allows the parties to draw upon a wider number of people with a wider range of knowledge and skills than happens under traditional bargaining.

- Where individuals who are impacted by the outcome experience having input into the outcome, they buy into the outcome and invest personal effort into making it work.
- It can reduce the need for first level management supervision where employees who participated in the development of new work arrange ments feel invested in living with and abiding by the new arrangements
- Where there are successful outcomes it demonstrates that it is possible to gain more from cooperation than from conflict, which reinforces the drive to cooperate.

CHAPTER SUMMARY

Interest-based bargaining is a specific approach to negotiation or problem solving. It is based on the assumption that it is possible for the interests of all parties to be satisfied. It is conducted in an agreed sequence with ground rules, agreed tools and techniques, and with the assistance of a facilitator. It requires advance joint training of the negotiating teams. A key objective of the process is to strengthen the working management-union relationship. As a form of dispute settlement it can be contrasted with power-based and rights-based approaches.

IBB will not work in all situations. It is not a panacea that can deliver easy results in difficult situations. Where, for example, management, employees and trade unions prefer to have an 'arms length' relationship with clearly delineated areas of responsibility, then adversarial bargaining is likely to be more useful to them. In assessing the usefulness of IBB it makes sense to think about the issues to be addressed, the parties con-cerned and their relationships, and the context in which the bargaining or problem solving will take place. Management and union representatives in Ireland have identified a number of situations in which they consider IBB might be of help to them and advocates of IBB have identified a range of 'generic' benefits that can accrue from its use.

The next chapter builds on this introduction to interest-based bargaining by defining and discussing the key building blocks of this approach – issues, positions, interests, options and standards.

-4-

DEFINING KEY INTEREST-BASED BARGAINING TERMS

'Interests are needs, desires, concerns and fears – the things one cares about or wants. They underlie people's positions – the tangible items they say they want'.

William L. Ury, Jeanne M. Brett and Stephen B. Goldberg (1988): Getting Disputes Resolved: Designing Systems to Cut the Costs of Conflict.

INTRODUCTION

WE FOCUS IN THIS CHAPTER in greater detail on the key concepts and terms in interest-based bargaining: issues, positions, interests, options and standards. At first sight these may look tricky but they are really straightforward. They become clear when parties get an opportunity to work with the concepts initially on a training course and then in practice. We define each of these terms using examples from the workplace and discuss them in some detail.

For convenience, this discussion assumes that there is a single union and management engaged in interest-based bargaining. In practice this will not always be the case. For example, many negotiations involve groups of unions. In cases such as this the parties need to tailor the IBB process to take account of the potential for unions to have different interests from one another. Needless to say this complicates matters just as it complicates adversarial bargaining to have several rather than one trade union involved.

ISSUES

An issue is a topic or problem that the parties want to address. Either management or trade unions can raise an issue. Conventionally issues raised by unions arise from meetings of their members and take the form of demands such as a claim for a pay increase of such and such an amount or for so many days additional annual leave or for some other benefit such as flexible working hours. In many cases union demands are inspired by what union members perceive as superior arrangements that colleagues or friends enjoy in other employments. Management demands or claims usually arise from some consideration of changes that are intended to make the organisation more productive or flexible or that are aimed at increasing revenues or reducing costs. It has already been seen that the industrial relations agenda has increasingly been dominated by managerial claims for changes arising from external market and other pressures.

In the previous chapter we saw that issues that are appropriate to interest-based bargaining will be issues that allow for solutions which benefit both parties or that allow for gains for one party that do not represent an equal sacrifice by the other party (Walton and McKersie, 1965). Does this mean that there are issues that, by definition, don't lend themselves to being handled through IBB? No, it doesn't. Management and unions have used IBB to address the full gamut of collective bargaining issues in the USA, as will be seen in Chapter 7.

At the same time, it is reasonable to suggest that some issues, such as money, are more difficult to handle simply because they are also, by their very nature, the most difficult issues to handle in positional or adversarial bargaining. Typically, money issues are handled later rather than earlier in IBB negotiations when the parties have developed strong relationships and skill in the IBB sequence. This is also common in adversarial bargaining where parties frequently conclude agreement on changes in work practices before tackling the tough money issues.

POSITIONS

A position is defined as one party's solution to an issue. So, if the issue is wage levels the union position is likely to be 'we want x% extra' and the management position is likely to be 'no, we cannot afford anything right now'. Adversarial bargaining, as already seen, revolves around the positions taken up early on by the parties to a negotiation. In adversarial bargaining, positions are the primary vehicle of communication and exchange between the negotiators. On each issue, each party has their position, their solution to that issue. Since the parties' positions on an issue typically are different, positional bargaining has a high probability of starting in disagreement.

Readers inclined toward the visual might think of a position as a brick and an interest as a pillow, each with both positive and negative charactertics. The positive characteristics of a brick (position) are that it is solid, angible, obvious, clear, and unambiguous. Its negative characteristics are that it is inflexible, resistant, hard, provocative, it can hurt those it is thrown at or dropped upon. The positive characteristics of a pillow (interest) are it is flexible, soft, accommodating, it wouldn't hurt anyone it is thrown at or dropped upon. Its negative characteristics are it is unclear, ambiguous, and subtle.

Interest-based bargaining challenges the traditional approach by not using positions, by not allowing either party to adopt or announce a position on any issue. For traditional bargainers this is a difficult concept to accept since taking positions is so much a part of the way we deal with each other.

INTERESTS

Interests are the underlying concerns, desires, needs that parties have about an issue. Parties usually have multiple interests rather than a single one. This provides a basis for generating a variety of different solutions to the issue being negotiated or the problem being solved. Interests are usually hidden behind positions and can be surfaced by asking the question 'why?' So, if a union wants a pay increase asking 'why' may lead to answers such as 'others in our industry are earning this and we want to be the same as them' or 'costs of living have increased and we need to keep up our standards of living'.

Typical management interests relating to wage level are 'we want to be able to recruit and retain the type of employees we need to be successful' or 'we need to be competitive and profitable to be able to pay high wages'.

Our values and our point of view sway our interests. What influences us and what we feel is important impact our interests. Our interests are not just based on what we like and want, but what we fear and avoid, what concerns and worries us. In that sense, interests can be negative. Our plans, goals and objectives also affect our interests. To successfully do interest-based bargaining, the parties must develop their skills to express their interests, hear the interests of others, find mutual interests and devise mutually acceptable ways of meeting these interests.

MUTUAL INTERESTS

Those interests that both parties have in common are called mutual interests. They are the richest source of the options needed in IBB. People using IBB for the first time are usually surprised at the high incidence of common interests around any given issue.

Mutual interest does not mean that the parties have an identical interest or a mathematically equal interest. One party may have a greater interest than the other, one may have a more immediate interest than the other, and yet the interest is mutual.

Stating interests carefully and listening attentively to how others state their interests are two skills that make the identification of mutual interests much easier.

SEPARATE BUT NON-CONFLICTING INTERESTS

Some interests are different, but do not cause conflict in the relationship. They are referred to here as separate, non-conflicting interests.

The separate, non-conflicting interests constitute a curious category. If one party is willing to interpret its interests more broadly, they might be able to convert a separate, non-conflicting interest into a mutual interest. For example, a union interest in financial security is a separate interest but it may not be in conflict with management's interests. While it does not initially appear to be a mutual interest, management could make it a mutual interest by interpreting their own interests more broadly. Management could do that by reasoning that union officials would be more secure, and therefore, easier to deal with if they spent less time collecting dues and worrying about finances.

Or a management interest around cost effectiveness might initially be a separate but non-conflicting interest. Unions might broaden their interests to encompass this one on the grounds that the job security and pay and conditions of their members depend on the overall efficiency of the organisation.

These types of interests provide options that can help to build relationships and trust between the parties. For example, if the party that does not share the interest can agree to an option that arises from that interest, the parties will have established a positive environment for other issues in the negotiation. This is not the same as one party saying to the other 'you owe me one' as is often heard in traditional bargaining. It is the creation of a positive environment for cooperation in bargaining by one side deliberately doing something to help the other side meet an interest.

SEPARATE AND CONFLICTING INTERESTS

Separate, conflicting interests can be a serious stumbling block in interest-based negotiations. But not as serious as might first appear. A traditional bargainer would assume that virtually all interests on all issues are conflicting. But a traditional bargainer's frame of reference is positional, and positions are by definition in conflict. However, here we are talking about interests.

This is not to suggest that there are no conflicting interests. There are. An employer interest in keeping costs down is in conflict with an employee interest in maximum compensation and a leisurely work pace. That is why the IBB process requires the parties to talk about more than a few interests on each issue. The more interests discussed on a given issue the better. The conflict of interests between keeping costs down and maximising compensation/comfort can be mitigated by the sharing of other interests, such as continuing employment and mutual survival, both of which are mutual interests. So in IBB, the parties' ability to express the maximum number of interests to each other is extremely important.

INDIVIDUAL INTERESTS

Up to this point, our discussion of separate and mutual interests has referred to group interests, as in union groups and management groups. Within such groups there are invariably individual interests. These interests may or may not be the same as the group interests. When these individual interests are different from the group interests, problems arise.

To make the IBB process work, groups and individuals must enter negotiations with a willingness to be persuaded. The consensus decision making technique, which is a key part of the P.A.S.T. model, requires this open-mindedness, this willingness to listen and be persuaded. This same decision-making process is used between individuals, within groups, and between union and management groups.

Union and management group interests do not disappear in the drive to discover or create mutual interests. The same is true within groups. Individual interests do not disappear in the drive to discover or create group consensus on interests within unions or management. In this sense, the individual's interests with respect to the group are like one group's interests with respect to mutual interests. Ultimately, the good-of-the-whole must be taken into account in determining which interests are going to be satisfied to their fullest, and which will not, in the final outcome of the negotiations. Sometimes this means that individuals drop commitment to their own interests in favour of commitment to a mutual interest that all parties can support such as the survival of the enterprise.

Since it is not rare for either union or management groups to find a resistant individual in their midst, teams often need skills and techniques for dealing with such situations.

ISSUES, POSITIONS AND INTERESTS

Let's take two classic collective bargaining issues to illustrate what we have been saying so far about issues, positions and interests. Two typical issues are wages and extended opening hours.

On an issue such as wages, trade unions and management usually take up opposing positions such as 'we want an increase of 5%' and 'we cannot afford any increase at all'. Because of lack of skill in IBB and old traditional bargaining habits, the union might state the issue as: a wage increase. Management, for the same reasons, might state the issue: a wage freeze for duration of the agreement. Neither of these ways of stating or framing the issue will facilitate IBB.

If the parties wanted to address wages using IBB, they would probably formulate or 'reframe' the issue for negotiation along the lines 'having remuneration that attracts and retains the workforce we need to be a successful organisation', see Box 4.1.

Instead of going head-to-head with opposing positions, the parties have created a basis for exploring their interests around the issue of remuneration that attracts and retains the workforce needed.

Defining Key Interest-Based Bargaining Terms

Likely union interests will be improving members' standards of living, keeping pay rates in line with comparable employments, and satisfying the members by delivering real benefits. Likely management interests will be keeping control of costs, being able to recruit and retain necessary staff, keeping within industry or national pay norms, and ensuring pay is in line with productivity.

BOX 4.1 ISSUE: HAVING A REMUNERATION SYSTEM THAT ATTRACTS
AND RETAINS THE WORKFORCE WE NEED

REFRAMED ISSUE	
We want to have a remuneration system that attracts and retains the workforce we need to be a successful organization	
Union Interests	**Management Interests**
• Improving members' living standards • Keeping pay in line with comparable employments • Satisfying members by delivering real benefits to them	• Keeping control of costs • Being able to recruit and retain necessary staff • Keeping within industry or national pay norms • Ensuring pay is in line with productivity

On issues such as extended business opening hours, management usually take a position such as 'we must extend the opening hours during lunch and in the afternoon'. Unions usually take up a position such as ' we are against extending opening hours unless we get such and such in return for cooperation'.

If the parties wanted to address extended opening hours using IBB, they would probably reframe the issue for negotiation along the lines 'having opening hours that meet the needs of our customers and our staff' as in Box 4.2 below. Instead of going head-to-head with opposing positions, the parties have created a basis for exploring their interests around the reframed issue.

Likely management interests will be delivering a better service and having satisfied customers, controlling costs, increasing revenues and having fewer complaints. Likely union interests will be ensuring members' hours of work are not increased, protecting staffing levels, protecting earnings, and having security if members are working late, and having good relations with customers.

BOX 4.2 ISSUE: HAVING OPENING HOURS THAT MEET CUSTOMER AND STAFF NEEDS

REFRAMED ISSUE	
We need to have opening hours that meet the needs of our customers and our staff	
Management Interests	**Union Interests**
• Delivering a better service and having satisfied customers • Controlling costs • Increasing revenues • Having fewer complaints	• Ensuring members' hours are not increased • Protecting staffing levels • Protecting earnings • Having security if members are working late • Having good relations with customers

By focusing on interests and not positions, the parties have now created a basis for looking at their interest lists to see to what extent there may be mutual interests, separate non-conflicting interests and conflicting interests. These interests will then form the basis of an effort to generate a number of options that might meet the principal interests.

In the wages scenario, the union interest in keeping pay in line with comparable employments looks fairly close to the management interest in keeping within industry or national pay norms. Indeed such a mutual interest frequently underpins joint pay benchmarking exercises. On the other hand, the union interest in satisfying members by delivering real benefits to them is not shared by management but they may not consider themselves in conflict with this interest providing it is not too much at their expense!

Improving members' standards of living and keeping control of costs look like conflicting interests and the challenge for the negotiators will be to see if they can generate options that are capable of satisfying the main interests of both parties.

In the extended hours scenario, the union is likely to share the management interests around better customer service, increasing revenues and reducing complaints, if not the costs interest. Management are likely to share the union interests around security and good relations with customers. Again, the challenge for both parties will be to see can they generate options to satisfy the mutual and separate interests.

DIFFERENCES BETWEEN POSITION AND INTEREST STATEMENTS

The difference between the position and the interest statements on these issues can be amplified by focusing on the characteristics of the statements. The position statements (e.g. 'we want an increase of 5%' and 'we cannot afford any increase at all') are definite and specific and provide the solutions to the issues. In many cases the solution is provided before the issue is understood, it precludes an open discussion around different possible solutions and it establishes the basis for an argument.

The interest statements are more flexible and less specific. They don't provide the solutions to the issues (e.g. controlling costs and protecting earnings). Instead they allow for open discussion and provide a basis for joint exploration of the issues.

Interest-based bargaining avoids that immediate lack of agreement and the subsequent urge to prepare for a fight. When the parties each state their position, a match between positions is unlikely. Whereas, when each party states a large number of interests, there is a high likelihood that a number of their interests will match as mutual interests. And while mutual interests do not resolve the issue, they provide the basis for options that can resolve the issue, and they set a tone for the parties to discuss the issue with a focus on agreement and mutuality, not on disagreement and the gap that separates the parties.

OPTIONS

An option is one of several possible solutions intended to meet or satisfy an interest on an issue. If only a single option is discussed it is the same as a position in which case the parties are really engaged in positional bargaining. Therefore, in IBB the parties are always seeking multiple options. When parties first begin to work with IBB, a good practice or rule of thumb is 'the more options on an issue, the better.'

STANDARDS

Since IBB is an interest-based process, it does not rely on power or rights to resolve bargaining issues. Instead standards are used for that purpose. A practical way of thinking about standards is to consider them as the characteristics of the option(s) that will lead them to be selected as the best solution or settlement. Asking the question 'why is this the best solution' is likely to be answered by the use of standards, e.g. it is the most beneficial, will be most acceptable, will work the best and so on.

The idea of a standard may initially seem foreign to most bargainers. The fact is most of us commonly use standards to make decisions but we seldom label them standards. For example, the decision on which route to drive when travelling home from work is based upon such factors as: how much time is available, whether there is a desire to relax or a need to hurry, the time of day and traffic patterns. The motorist can use any one or more of these factors or standards to make the decision.

The decision made by a diner while reading a restaurant menu involves the use of standards, although the diner would not say that standards determine what was ordered. In making the selection, the diner considers his or her budget, the listed prices, personal likes and dislikes, stomach signals on the extent of hunger, any special dietary requirements and the restaurant's reputation. All of these are standards that influence the decision made by the diner.

Another example of using standards is an angler deciding which fish to keep and which to throw back. Each fish caught is an option requiring a decision. The angler bases the decision on the size and weight of the fish, whether the fish is edible or not, the license laws and the number and type of fish he or she has already caught. The angler can use any of these factors or standards in deciding which fish to keep.

Many organisations are accustomed to standards. Science, engineering and health care organizations use standards extensively in all of their work. Quality control inspectors apply standards on the work and performance of others within an organisation. Employees from organisations that routinely use standards can easily become comfortable with using standards in bargaining.

Standards in negotiations are not scientific; they lack the precision of the laboratory. They are more of a guide or an aid to decision makers. Because they are more subjective than objective, they require discussion and consensus as they are being applied. Frequently, as some of the illustrations above have shown, several standards are used together in making the decision because one standard is not sufficient.

There are a number of different ways of selecting and applying standards and these will be discussed in Chapter 5.

CHAPTER SUMMARY

Issues are the topics or problems for bargaining or problem solving. Positions are one party's solutions to those problems or issues. In adversarial bargaining, arguments are used to explain and justify positions. Interests are the needs and concerns that people have about an issue. The ideas and concepts embedded in positional arguments are very similar to the ideas and concepts in interest statements. The purpose of an argument, however, is to win agreement on a position and it is frequently met with resistance and counter argument from the other side.

In contrast, the purpose of interest statements and discussions is to inform, to seek commonality and create a dialogue between the parties. The tone of interest discussions is reflective, seeking understanding, and cooperation. The result of interest discussions is identification of mutual interests, appreciation of separate interests, and mutual education of both parties. There will inevitably be a mix of mutual, separate but non-conflicting interests and conflicting interests in complex negotiation and problem solving.

Interest-based bargaining seeks to generate a number of possible options for satisfying the principal interests of both parties. Rather than using power to decide which options will form the basis of settlement, the parties agree to use objective standards as a means of judging the options.

Having outlined these key definitions we can move on in the next chapter to describe in detail how the interest-based bargaining sequence works in practice.

-5-

THE INTEREST-BASED BARGAINING SEQUENCE

'The success in IBB at each step of the process depends on choices made in prior steps and all of these process choices add up, having a powerful impact on substantive outcomes. In other words, process matters.'
Joel Cutcher-Gershenfeld (2003): How Process Matters: A Five-Phase Model for Examining Interest Based Bargaining.

INTRODUCTION

WE DESCRIBE IN DETAIL in this chapter how interest-based bargaining works. Firstly, we discuss the practical steps that parties need to take to prepare for IBB. These are called the pre-bargaining steps. In particular we focus on how parties should deal with their constituents before commencing bargaining or problem solving, how they should gather information and how they should develop opening statements.

These steps are essential if the new approach is to have a better than average chance of working to the satisfaction of the parties. Then we discuss the IBB sequence itself which has five steps: meeting to agree and focus each issue, developing interests around that issue, generating options to meet the interests, agreeing on what standards to apply in selecting options, and reaching consensus on the best options.

This discussion assumes the parties have discussed and agreed why they want to develop interest-based bargaining and have put other supports in place such as facilitation, ground rules for negotiations and joint training. These are important elements of successful IBB. This discussion also assumes a situation in which there is a single union and a single employer. It also assumes that there is an external facilitator helping the group.

In order to highlight the differences between the nuts and bolts of IBB and adversarial bargaining we begin with a short discussion of the adversarial bargaining sequence.

ADVERSARIAL BARGAINING SEQUENCE

Interest-based bargaining can appear complicated with its different steps compared to adversarial bargaining, which appears more straightforward. We hope to show that IBB is not complicated once bargaining teams have mastered the basic concepts and have had the opportunity to practice the sequence during training.

Even though there are no written rules for adversarial bargaining – apart from whatever might be stated in grievance procedures or codes of conduct – it too has a number of steps that combine to form an adversarial bargaining sequence. The key steps include:

- Preparation for bargaining by identifying issues, preparing positions and fallback positions and developing supporting evidence and arguments. Small negotiating teams working with wider groups of management and union constituents usually carry out these preparations.
- One side notifies the other of its desire to negotiate or they agree together that negotiations are necessary
- A first meeting takes place and the parties exchange opening positions
- Further meetings are scheduled to address an agreed list of issues
- Discussion of issues takes place in some logical sequence
- The bargaining follows a pattern of proposal and counter-proposal and argument/counter-argument
- There are likely to be informal contacts between the lead negotiators to explore ideas and to discuss possible concessions and other moves
- As the deadline for agreement comes nearer the parties may agree to have more meetings
- The negotiators brief their constituents as necessary
- The parties may 'up the ante' on each other through pressure tactics and there may be some form of industrial action
- The parties may use a mediator to help bridge the gaps between them or, less typically, they may agree to refer their differences to a third party for arbitration.
- Finally, the parties narrow the gap down by making late concessions to each other and a settlement is reached that reflects the relative power at that time of the negotiating parties.

These steps, which only give the baldest outline of what happens in adversarial bargaining, are not written down and described as the 'adversarial bargaining sequence' but there are few significant negotiations that don't include most of them. Against this background, then, what is different about the interest-based bargaining sequence?

INTEREST-BASED BARGAINING: PRE-BARGAINING STEPS

There are two phases to the IBB sequence that we are recommending in this book. The first phase, which is about preparation, happens before the formal bargaining or problem solving commences and the second phase is the actual bargaining sequence itself. Preparation is especially important in IBB because the bargaining teams need to ensure that their constituents understand and support the process and because they need to ensure that their mandate in going into the bargaining is compatible with an interest-based approach rather than being framed in traditional adversarial or positional terms. Before bargaining commences, therefore, a number of important things need to happen.

CONSTITUENTS' SUPPORT

Both management and trade unions need to ensure that their constituents fully understand and support the bargaining process, especially if it is being used for the first time. This will require separate and perhaps joint meetings or workshops at which constituents have opportunities to tease out how IBB works and what the implications for them might be.

In particular it will be important to address how issues are presented, i.e. as interests and not as positions, and how ratification will be effected, i.e. when and how decision-making procedures will be activated. Union members may want assurances that they will have the same right to ballot on important outcomes affecting them as they enjoy under adversarial collective bargaining.

Both sides need to recognise that in developing a list of issues, they are dealing with constituents' expectations and they should not distort them. They should, however, help constituents to be as realistic as possible.

BARGAINING TEAMS

Bargaining teams tend to take three forms. Firstly, there are the conventional types of bargaining teams found in adversarial bargaining. These tend to comprise of full-time union officials, local union representatives such as shop stewards and industrial relations managers and line managers involved in whatever issue happens to be on the table.

Secondly, there are bargaining teams comprised of management and union personnel who are drawn more from the partnership arena than from adversarial bargaining. These are likely to include line managers and local union representatives as well as individual employees drafted in because of an interest or knowledge in the issue under discussion. Such groups may or may not be supplemented by full-time union officials and industrial relations managers, depending on the issues on the table. This type of bargaining team is likely to be established to resolve a particular dispute or solve a particular problem that has come up through the partnership system.

In such cases it is becoming common to use the term 'interest-based problem solving' rather than 'interest-based bargaining' to describe what the parties are doing.

Thirdly, there may be extant groups such as a joint management-union working group or a partnership committee, which decides to use interest-based bargaining as a working methodology to address a particular issue or problem.

It will be important to ensure that bargaining teams or problem solving teams include individuals who have knowledge and expertise in the issue or problem being addressed as well as individuals who are representative of the groups affected. It is also important to have the key players or decision-makers directly involved so that the bargaining teams are not constantly running back to base for approval on developments (Stepp et al, 2003). Size matters too: given the strong emphasis placed on communications, active listening, brainstorming etc in the IBB approach it will be important not to have very large groups where this can be avoided. Ten to twelve is probably a desirable size range but circumstances may dictate higher or lower numbers.

AGREEING ON THE AGENDA

The agenda may comprise a single issue or many. There are a number of ways of stating issues, as seen earlier, that can complicate the task of developing an agreed upon list. An issue can be stated in a word or short phrase, for example: 'staffing' or 'staffing problems.' Or that same issue can be stated more completely in a phrase such as: 'staffing the emergency room with qualified nurses on holidays and weekends.' It's better to have a short but comprehensive statement for each of the issues to be negotiated.

Agreeing on the bargaining agenda is critical. In some cases, especially when IBB is being used for the first time, parties are likely to want to try it out on soft or moderately difficult issues rather than on the types of issues that have proven to be very difficult to resolve in the past. This also happens in adversarial bargaining, as seen earlier in the case of money issues, where parties frequently 'park' difficult issues until late in the process in the expectation that successfully addressing less significant issues will prepare the ground for later handling of more difficult ones.

We have seen already that adversarial bargaining agendas take the form of positional claims or demands. With IBB the agenda needs to consist of issues that are framed in broader terms that allow for the identification of interests and the generation of options. If constituents have presented issues in the form of positions or demands then the negotiators will have to work with them to convert the position statements into interest statements. This might be more easily said than done if the constituents only have a vague understanding of IBB or if their commitment to it is only skin-deep, as it may be first time around.

If a mandate is narrowly framed then the scope for considering a wide range of options during subsequent brainstorming may be highly constrained (Cutcher-Gershenfeld, 2003). Hence it is important to give sufficient time and effort to securing a solid degree of understanding and support among constituents in the first instance. At the end of the day, however, negotiators have to take the mandate they are given.

GATHERING INFORMATION

Some parties find it useful to examine their list of issues to determine which ones might require additional information before starting negotiations. Frequently sub-committees are assigned to gather the needed information. This will be particularly important where parties are addressing complex issues (Stepp et al, 2003).

Using sub-committees or joint working groups can help to graft the IBB process on to existing partnership processes, for example by asking managers and union representatives with past experience of joint working to carry out research for the main bargaining teams. Issues of a similar nature that have been clustered are frequently handled in a series. Some issues will only be handled when data or reports from a subcommittee are available.

TAKING JOINT TRAINING

Interest-based bargaining teams are always jointly trained in the bargaining sequence and the tools and techniques used. To participate in training that is not joint is contrary to the IBB approach, it suggests that the parties are arming themselves against the other side. Separate training in interest-based bargaining must be avoided.

In the first instance, it will be helpful to the IBB process for the facilitator to design and deliver a briefing on IBB for the bargaining teams and their constituencies. This hour or two long session will provide an opportunity for the facilitator to explain IBB and answer questions. Usually, briefings are conducted separately for trade unions and management to allow the 'hard questions' to be asked. If either party feels a need for greater efforts to convince their constituency of the merits of IBB, the facilitator can help with written materials, additional conversations or consulting. Following the briefings, and other efforts if used, it will become apparent whether or not the constituents and the bargaining teams approve of using the interest-based approach.

Effective training should provide ample opportunities for parties to tease out and discuss the principles, assumptions, tools and techniques of IBB and to relate this to their own experiences of adversarial bargaining and other forms of joint problem solving.

The training should also provide an opportunity for the parties to practice taking an issue through the entire bargaining or problem solving sequence. In this way, the parties can get a real sense for what it is going to be like to use an interest-based approach. The training may also be used to decide which issues to tackle in the first round of actual bargaining as well as for establishing ground rules and practical arrangements around where and when to meet, facilitation arrangements, who contacts who about meetings, who takes charge of documents etc.

It is important for everyone who is going to take part in the bargaining or problem solving to take part in the training otherwise those who do not will not share whatever 'common understanding' about interest-based bargaining emerges from the training. The training may also provide the parties with the opportunity to see if they are satisfied or not with the knowledge, attitude and skills of the facilitator. If they decide to go ahead and take an interest-based approach, they can then decide whether to invite this facilitator back or to look for someone else.

AN EXAMPLE OF JOINT TRAINING

Box 5.1 outlines the approach to training in interest-based problem solving adopted by the management and trade unions in HSE-South West Area.

BOX 5.1 TRAINING FOR INTEREST-BASED PROBLEM SOLVING

The management and unions in HSE-South West Area, through their partnership committee, decided to train several hundred local managers and union representatives in interest-based problem solving. They wanted to use the principles of 'Getting to Yes', and 'Interest-Based Problem Solving'.

They saw this as an alternative to adversarial bargaining. Their main aim was to reduce the non-value adding time spent in adversarial negotiations and to increase the commitment to value adding organisational activity through problem solving.

Some twenty managers, union representatives and employees applied and were interviewed for places on a six-day training course. The six days were divided in two parts.

The first part was a three-day introduction to interest-based bargaining or problem solving based on the PAST Model. The participants took an issue through the five steps in the interest-based sequence and reviewed at each stage what it was like to be using such a different methodology for addressing a problem that would in the normal course be handled through adversarial bargaining.

The second part of the training was a further three days aimed at developing presentation and training skills. Participants worked in pairs to prepare and deliver information and skills sessions along the lines of the ones they themselves had taken part in on the first three-day session. In this way, the full group had the opportunity to work on the delivery of a full training programme on interest-based bargaining or problem solving.

DEVELOPING GROUND RULES

Either during training or shortly afterwards the parties discuss and agree the types of ground rules that they consider will help them to be successful at the interest-based approach. The idea of ground rules of an explicit type may be somewhat foreign to many negotiators used to adversarial bargaining. It should be borne in mind, however, that just as the adversarial process follows a certain sequence – albeit one that is not usually written down for bargaining teams to follow – it also works in accordance with certain ground rules.

Because IBB requires the parties to follow a different sequence and to behave quite differently – being open about interests, sharing information, avoiding positions etc – it is useful to have some ground rules that will help to keep parties 'on the straight and narrow' when using the process. Some sample ground rules that have been found helpful in a variety of situations are set out in Chapter 6.

PREPARING OPENING STATEMENTS

Setting the tone for interest-based bargaining is critically important. When the parties meet for their first formal session, it is usual to begin with opening statements that set a positive and constructive tone that will get the bargaining or problem solving off to a good start.

It is helpful if parties use this opportunity to say why they have decided to use the IBB process as opposed to adversarial bargaining. Opening statements are usually short and to the point. Opening statements are a deliberate effort to stay away from the type of conflictual openings that typify adversarial bargaining. When thinking about what to say to the other side it is useful for a party to think: what would I like to hear them saying to us? And then formulate an opening statement along the desired lines.

Obviously, the parties avoid presenting an opening position or a set of demands. They also avoid trying to create a 'high noon' atmosphere reminiscent of certain types of adversarial bargaining. Instead they commit themselves to the IBB process and in particular to being open to the best solution the group can reach.

THE FIVE BARGAINING STEPS

Having prepared the ground with constituents, having made all the necessary practical arrangements and having made the opening statements it is now time to begin the actual bargaining or problem solving sequence.

The sequence used in the PAST Model has five separate steps as set out in Diagram 5.1 below.

DIAGRAM 5.1 INTEREST BASED BARGAINING SEQUENCE

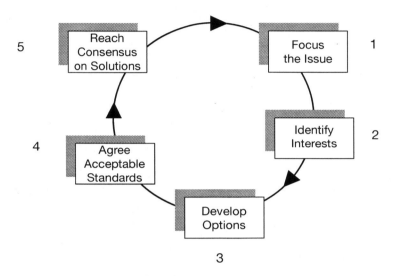

The parties go through each step with each of the issues on their agenda. The importance of having a formal model is to give parties, especially parties using the process for the first time, a sequence and a set of tools and ground rules to help them to avoid slipping into adversarial bargaining.

Firstly, the parties come together in a joint session to clarify or focus the issue. Secondly, they identify their separate and common interests. They usually identify their own interests in separate caucus meetings and then share these interests in a joint session.

Thirdly, they develop options, usually together, to satisfy as many of the interests as possible. Fourthly, they develop together agreed standards or criteria to evaluate these options. Fifthly, they apply these standards in separate and/or joint sessions and arrive at a consensus on the preferred options. Each of the five steps is important in its own right and success at each step depends on what happened at previous steps.

They then write up their agreement in whatever form makes sense for the issue concerned: a memorandum of understanding, an exchange of letters, a collective bargaining agreement, a management notice etc.

It can be useful at the end of each step to spend a few minutes summarising what has happened, thus providing an opportunity for bargaining team members to comment on what happened and then to confirm briefly what is going to happen at the next step and what process the parties will be using.

Once the parties have become accustomed to the new assumptions and behaviours they may modify the sequence to suit themselves.

The parties might work through the entire sequence in an extended bargaining or problem solving session lasting a day or two or they might meet weekly or fortnightly for a few hours at a time as in adversarial bargaining: it all depends on the urgency of the problem and the availability of the parties.

IBB is very demanding and a day of negotiations should not normally exceed eight hours; marathon sessions should never be attempted (Stepp et al, 1998). Experience from the USA suggests that IBB does not take longer than adversarial bargaining when all the separate and joint sessions are taken into account.

STEP ONE: FOCUSING THE ISSUE

When the parties have made their opening statements on the first issue they want to handle, they then need to focus or frame this issue. They do this in a joint session. This simply means scoping out why the issue has arisen, why it needs to be resolved and what the broad parameters are. For example, if the issue relates to customer service, is it customer service in all parts of the organisation or in a particular unit or place? If the issue is absenteeism what hard data is available to frame the discussion? Why do the parties reckon this issue needs to be tackled etc?

It is important to stay away from positions at this stage. One way to avoid the tendency to embed a position in an issue is to state issues in the form of a question since questions usually do not include answers or positions. If, for example, the issue relates to extended opening hours, rather than simply having 'extended opening hours' or 'introducing extended opening hours' as the issue, it can be helpful to word the issue as 'how might we introduce extended opening hours to everyone's satisfaction?' Or if changing the holiday rostering arrangements is the issue this might be worded as 'how can we change the holiday rostering arrangements so that more staff can be accommodated while meeting the needs of clients?'

This is like problem definition and involves making sure that everyone is 'on the same page' before getting into identifying interests and generating options. If the parties need a lot of data to resolve the problem and if it emerges at this early stage that they simply don't have the data then it will probably be necessary to backtrack and gather that data for joint consideration before moving to the next step.

A member of one of the bargaining teams or an external facilitator will flip chart the discussion and help keep the group focused on the immediate task which is focusing or scoping the issue as opposed to looking at interests or options. The chart paper should be titled and dated for later use.

STEP TWO: IDENTIFYING INTERESTS

The next step is for the parties to identify their interests around this one issue. To make IBB work, bargainers must suppress the urge to quickly decide on a position on an issue and argue for it. Instead bargainers must start with the belief that the issue can be solved but they don't yet know what the answer is.

Then they must talk about their interests as completely as possible, listen to the interests of the other side, and work through the IBB sequence. This is not to suggest that people don't have ideas in their heads as to what their preferred solutions are: they simply don't put them on the table early on and they try to be as open as possible to other alternative solutions.

Probably on the first issue, the parties will be most comfortable identifying their own interests in caucus or side meeting before moving to a joint session to discuss and seek mutual interests. If interests are discussed in caucus, the parties should not only identify their own interests, they should spend some time attempting to anticipate the interests of the other side. This will help them hear and understand the other side's interests during the ensuing joint session. They chart their interests on a flip chart for bringing back to the plenary session.

When they have identified their own interests, the parties come together to report them to each other. This takes the form of an open discussion with the two lists of interests pinned to the walls or on separate flip charts. It is helpful if team members probe each other's interests for clarification and understanding. Useful questions to ask are: 'why do you have that interest?' and 'what information or experience lies behind that interest?'

Interest statements cannot, however, be rejected, objected to, or disagreed with by the other party. As seen earlier, interests are like feelings; they are the party's own. They don't require justification, whereas positions require, even demand, justification.

SHARING INFORMATION ABOUT INTERESTS

Identifying and sharing information about the parties' respective interests is a crucial part of the IBB approach. Talking about an interest in an open and accepting environment can help the parties to develop a new perspective on that interest.

An example of the latter might be a negative interest, such as fear. A union negotiating on the issue of work restructuring might express a negative interest, such as a fear of job losses. That fear, that interest, might be mitigated when the management shares information about the large expected increase in workloads arising from providing additional services. That new information might provide a new perspective that encourages a change in the union's interest statement, or a lowering of the priority of that interest compared with other union interests on the work restructuring issue.

It will be clear that this is a much more open process than positional bargaining where parties conceal their true interests behind exaggerated and even fake positions. The norm in traditional bargaining is to share only that information which will help your position and/or hurt the other side's position. For traditional bargainers, information is seen as power; they use it as a weapon.

MUTUAL INTERESTS

Mutual interests are the most comfortable interests to externalise. But with any interest, the parties will not know if the interest is mutual until they have shared information about that interest. If the open sharing of interest information is not the norm for the two bargaining teams, they are taking a risk when they share information. Hence the importance of having a facilitator and ground rules that can support openness.

In identifying mutual interests, the parties should assure themselves to a sufficient degree that the interest is truly mutual and they should avoid trying to force issues together as being mutual in order to oblige each other or to appear more cooperative. For example, if one party has an interest in apples and the other an interest in oranges, it is probably sufficient to agree they have a mutual interest in fruit rather than 'being nice' and pretending that they both have a mutual interest in apples and oranges.

SEPARATE INTERESTS

It is important to identify and discuss interests that are not mutual and that are also not conflicting. Simply identifying, explaining, acknowledging and then moving on can be helpful in establishing an atmosphere of mutual respect. It also brings a strong element of realism into the bargaining or problem solving when separate interests are identified. Management, for example, might articulate an interest around cost savings and the union side might say that they understand why the management have that interest but decline to have it as a mutual interest.

CONFLICTING INTERESTS

Needless to say, parties will from time to time have sharply conflicting interests. In talking about conflicting interests, it is important to remember what an interest is and is not. The party who listens to and hears the other party's conflicting interest might not like what they hear and they may be concerned about how that interest can be met but they are not being asked to agree with the interest or to act on it. The expression of a conflicting interest is merely one party's statement of concern about an issue. The party expressing the interest may hope that the other party will do something about it, but there is no obligation on them in IBB to do so.

As indicated earlier, IBB is not a way of avoiding differences. Instead, this approach recognises that different interests and viewpoints are inevitable and even desirable in that their expression represents a degree of honesty not usually present in adversarial bargaining. Also, having differences can generate a creative tension that strengthens the attempts to arrive at mutually acceptable solutions.

DISGUISING POSITIONS AS INTERESTS

A difficulty in interest-based bargaining is with negotiators who attempt to disguise their positions by using words that appear to be interest statements. For example, by preceding a position statement with: 'We have an interest in staying competitive in a very difficult product market, and therefore, we feel the employees should pay a larger percentage of the pension premium' does not convert it into an interest.

In cases like this it is helpful if group members challenge each other with questions such as 'is that an interest or a position that you have just expressed?' Sometimes it takes time for some people to grasp the difference between an interest and a position.

Persistently or deliberately dressing up a position in a new word package to make it sound like an interest is likely to be unhelpful to the process. Such tactics are not interest-based bargaining, and the other party will recognise it as such. Interest-based bargaining is a genuine and sincere effort to express interests and hear the other side's interests as a basis for developing and considering all possible options.

HIDDEN AGENDAS

A difficult problem with individual interests (and occasionally group interests) occurs when an individual (or a group) is not candid about an interest. This lack of candour is often referred to as a hidden or private agenda. To make the IBB process work, individuals must not only be open minded and willing to be persuaded, they must also be open and candid about their individual interests.

If an individual does not express his or her interests openly and completely to members of the group, but instead, uses those unstated interests to block progress in the negotiations, the process will not succeed. Everyone in the negotiation must be aware of the relevant interests. Anyone who holds back such information is manipulating the process and engaging in traditional bargaining.

STEP THREE: DEVELOPING OPTIONS

The next step is to develop options or ways of satisfying the interests generated. The main source of the ideas generated is likely to be the mutual interests since these represent the common ground between the parties. It is important to bear in mind that the separate and conflicting interests remain on the chart paper and may also be the source of ideas.

In some versions of IBB the parties delete the separate and conflicting interests before generating options. We think this is a mistake. Asking parties to drop important interests is quite positional: it is asking them to make a concession. Also, it is likely to strike them as unrealistic to do this: think of a management being asked to drop an interest around cost effectiveness because it wasn't a mutual interest or a union being asked to drop an interest around job security for the same reason.

One of the strengths of IBB is precisely that it allows parties to work on all interests and not just mutual ones. In IBB, as seen earlier, it frequently happens that a lot of the energy and creativity comes from trying to generate options that can meet separate and even conflicting interests.

It is critical for the parties to work together, not in caucuses when generating options. If they attempt to do even part of this step in caucuses, they will develop union options and management options which are likely to be very much like positions. When that occurs, the parties will not be able to use standards and reach consensus later.

To avoid the temptation to caucus, the parties should remember: 1) the process doesn't work once positions are introduced, even if done very subtly; and 2) this step involves creating a range of possible options on a 'without prejudice' basis within an understanding that 'nothing is agreed until everything is agreed'.

BRAINSTORMING

The creative use of brainstorming is crucial. The emphasis in developing options is on the creation of as many options as possible, and on not judging the options. Judging will come later. The reason for emphasizing the quantity and not the quality of options is to get as many ideas available for consideration as possible. It is useful to remember that options can be either substantive (capable of being implemented immediately or soon) or procedural (a process such as a review that can lead to substantive options later). Sometimes brainstorming will stay focused on one or the other. When that happens, someone needs to ask if options of the other type are needed.

Brainstorming options openly does not come easy to many traditional bargainers. It involves risks. There are risks in making suggestions that one might want to withdraw or amend later and there are risks in making suggestions without prior discussion with colleagues, something that rarely happens in adversarial bargaining. Where trust is still developing and where parties are doing this for the first time then this might be a slow, deliberate process rather than the fast and energetic process often associated with brainstorming. The important thing is that parties stick with the process and that they 'trust it' to produce good results for them.

The parties generate options while looking at and considering all the interests together rather than by considering each interest on its own. The facilitator can be very helpful at this stage by encouraging, challenging, energising and otherwise helping the group to come up with as many suggestions as possible. When ideas are running short the facilitator may ask the group to check the lists of interests one more time to see are there any important interests for which no options have been generated.

Some of the ideas will be poor. But even those ideas can trigger and provoke other ideas that might provide needed options.

An example of creating options may help here. If the parties have a mutual interest in reducing absenteeism, some of their options could include: reducing annual leave entitlements, reducing sick leave entitlements, financial rewards for no absences in a given period, stricter rules for production of medical certificates, referral to company doctor, more flexible working hours, a joint union-management study committee to identify roots of the problem, hiring consultants and others. The first two options, and maybe others on the list, are poor if not absurd options. Other options listed may be

good, or may provide a basis for other, better options. The judging of that comes later when standards are applied.

While brainstorming is the primary technique for creating options, it is not the only way. At least three other methods for creating options and/or aiding brainstorming are available. These are benchmarking or best practice, study groups and bringing in experts.

BENCHMARKING

Benchmarking or best practice involves examining the innovative practices and solutions of other organisations. This is usually done by a combination of site visits, consultation with other organisations, and reviewing written materials. This work is done jointly with management and union representatives participating fully through sub committees or working groups. It will also involve contacts with union representatives and managers at the sites being visited.

Typically benchmarking is used on relatively complex issues, e.g. issues involving major changes such as work redesign and restructuring. For example, a group that is addressing significant changes in work practices may want to know how similar work is done in other organizations that they would rank highly in terms of performance. Or if a group was addressing the pay and conditions of employees they might want to benchmark their own arrangements against other comparable organisations in their industry or sector.

Benchmarking is not a new idea in Ireland. There are many examples of its use in joint management-union examinations of working practices, technologies, staffing levels, as well as in pay negotiations.

STUDY GROUPS

This process involves collecting and analysing information within an organisation to better understand the problem and possible solutions. Once the data has been analysed, options can be developed by the joint study committee for the bargaining teams to consider or the findings from the study group may be brought back to the bargaining teams who would then generate options themselves

HEARING FROM EXPERTS

In IBB the more technical expertise available within the bargaining teams the better, but it is unrealistic to think that all the necessary expertise can always be available in this way. Experts can provide the bargaining teams with the information and education needed on a given issue. The joint bargaining team can bring in experts from either management or trade unions or an outside expert to share their expertise. In that context the bargaining team members can ask the expert for their ideas or opinions.

It will be important to have agreement on the choice of experts otherwise the benefit of the expertise may be lost as one side or the other may consider them to be biased in favour of the side that suggested them. The practice of having agreed experts, especially around financial and other technical matters, is increasingly common in Ireland. In many cases, bodies such as the LRC and Labour Court appoint such experts to assist parties to resolve issues that are going through an adversarial bargaining process.

REFINING THE LIST OF OPTIONS

At the end of the brainstorming session, things can get a bit messy if there are large numbers of options (which is, needless to say, a good situation to have) and if parties have no experience of IBB. A good brainstorming session should yield several pages of flip-charted suggestions.

It makes sense, therefore, before plunging into decisions about what standards to apply to see if it is possible to reduce the number of options or to order them in some way. This is not the same as evaluating the options.

Reducing should only take place on the basis of eliminating duplicate options or of amalgamating options that are closely related to each other. Or parties might like to cluster the options in some logical way, for example into lists of substantive and procedural options or into lists of 'short', 'medium' and 'long term' options or whatever other approach makes sense in the particular circumstances. Using different colours to identify clusters or categories of options can be very effective and is simple to do.

STEP FOUR: DECIDING AND APPLYING STANDARDS

In this step, the parties are trying to reduce the impact of power in their relationship and shift the basis of decision-making to standards that are fair and mutually agreed upon. The parties sit together, not in caucuses, and look at the lists of options that they have generated together. It may be that experienced bargaining teams already have an established set of standards and an established way of applying them. In this case they will quickly move on to the next step having confirmed how they are going to do it. If not, there are at least three separate, but related, methods available to them. These are:

- Applying the three basic standards of 'feasible', 'beneficial', 'acceptable'
- Scoring options using a 0-10 rating
- Developing their own list of standards for the issue in hand

Any one of these methods can be used alone or bargaining teams may opt to combine some of them together. Our experience has been that the use of the three basic standards works best in most situations.

THREE BASIC STANDARDS: FEASIBLE, BENEFICIAL, AND ACCEPTABLE

This method relies on testing each option in sequence against three basic standards one at a time. This is like using three sieves with large, medium and small holes to ensure only the best gravel or flour remains. Feasible means that the option can actually be implemented, i.e. there is no legal, financial or other impediment to its implementation. Beneficial means that the option satisfies one or more interests. Acceptable means that the wider management and union constituents as well as the bargaining team members are likely to consider it acceptable. Parties can use the type of grid shown in Diagram 5.2 for convenience using the flip chart.

DIAGRAM 5.2 USING A GRID TO HELP IN EVALUATING OPTIONS

Options	Feasible	Beneficial	Acceptable

Thus, each option or grouping of options is examined intensively to see if it has feasibility in all of its important particulars. If not, it is discarded. If the consensus is that the option meets the test of feasibility, it moves to the second stage, an analysis of how well the option achieves benefits by meeting interests. The third stage is an examination of acceptability to management and constituents. If, for some reason, although the option is both feasible and beneficial, there is some serious question as to its acceptability, the group may find it useful to spend some effort to find a way of overcoming the acceptability flaw.

If the option passes all three tests it becomes part of the 'tentative agreement' of the group unless succeeding options are found to provide better solutions and are incompatible with the option just analyzed. Agreement to move an option to the next stage or to tentative agreement is always made by a consensus of the entire group.

OPTION RATING

This method provides the bargaining teams with an opportunity to rate the options in caucus meetings as well as in a joint session. The parties rate each option on a scale of 0-10 with 0 meaning the option is of no value and 10 meaning the option is the perfect solution. A 5 ranking means that the option has some merit but needs to be amended to become acceptable. A ranking of 6 or more usually means that the option is acceptable. The parties can use a grid like the one shown below in Diagram 5.3 drawn on a flip chart as a convenient way of doing this and as a means of reporting their conclusions to each other.

When the parties have ranked the options separately they come together in joint session and report back their decisions and the reasoning behind them. This usually leads to some discussion to see if the option might be amended to get a higher ranking if it got a low one from one party and a high one from the other. There may even be some trade-offs around options that are highly valued by one party only.

DIAGRAM 5.3 OPTION RATING GRID

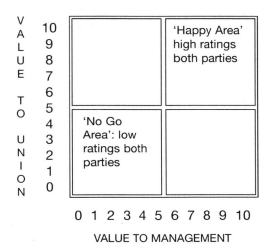

VALUE TO MANAGEMENT

DEVELOPING OWN STANDARDS

The parties may consider that they need to have standards that are specific to their circumstances. If so, they use brainstorming to generate a list of such standards. They need to have a consensus on whatever standards they decide to use. They may also choose from a list of 'generic' standards such as feasible, acceptable, fair, cost effective, flexible, mutually beneficial etc.

Some serious difficulties can arise if the list of standards gets high. The more standards being used the more cumbersome the effort becomes and the greater the likelihood of parties having different interpretations of what the standards mean. Also, it begs the question as to whether some or all of the standards have to be met for an option to qualify for agreement. This is why we recommend the use of the three basic standards of feasible, beneficial and acceptable.

STEP FIVE: USING CONSENSUS TO DEVELOP SOLUTIONS

In this step, working in a joint session and using consensus decision making, the parties test the options they have developed against the standards they have chosen in order to determine which options best address their interests on that issue. It is the satisfaction of interest that provides gain so probing the link between interests and options is desirable. If the list of options is extensive, it can be reduced to a manageable length by combining any redundant options, and by eliminating any options that meet none of the standards.

Next the bargainers discuss each option in the light of each standard to eliminate even more options. The parties need to develop this step to fit their preferred way of working together. Some parties find it useful to initially move quickly through the list with a minimum of discussion and label the options using the labels and categories set out in Box 5.2 below:

BOX 5.2 WAYS OF CATEGORISING OPTIONS

N = eliminated by one or more standards
Y = not eliminated by any standard
MB = maybe if not clearly an N or Y
IC = if combined with other options, it could meet the standards.

Then a more detailed discussion of the remaining options can focus discussion on further reducing or combining options. Once the bargainers become skilled with the process, and the norm in the bargaining supports cooperation and joint solution seeking, this step will become very creative.

For example, with the union and management teams working as one group, and with the lists of interests, options and standards displayed on the wall in front of the entire group, one member of the group might suggest: 'With a minor revision, the fourth and seventh options could be combined to read as follows….and that new option would address six of the eight mutual interests and all three standards would be met.' Following a few questions by group members, another member might suggest a further modification that would help the new option meet an additional mutual interest. As more discussion follows, consensus emerges.

When the parties reach consensus on the issue, they might assign a subcommittee to develop the necessary formal language for that issue. The subcommittee can report back to the bargaining committees at their next negotiating session.

The parties can then take up the next issue and go through the IBB sequence again. If the parties cannot reach consensus after a reasonable period on an issue, the issue can be set aside by mutual agreement for later discussion or it can be referred to a joint subcommittee for further examination or perhaps for further information while the parties move on to another issue.

If the parties are negotiating a number of issues at one time rather than a single issue, then it is likely that they will end up with some settled and some unsettled issues. The unsettled issues can be grouped in categories based on similarities of issues or interests. For example, all the money issues can be grouped. Then negotiations can be focused on a group of issues. A package of options can be fashioned to address all the issues in the group.

Unlike traditional negotiations, in which settled issues are almost never reopened for discussion, IBB does not foreclose that possibility in this final stage of settlement. Consistent with the assumption that the parties should help each other win, this final stage of negotiation provides the opportunity to revisit any issue for further discussion in developing the final package.

Occasionally the parties will make proposals to each other during this Step. Such proposals differ from traditional bargaining because they are based on an extensive sharing of information about interests, frank discussion about options, a willingness to use mutual gain as a standard for decision making rather than power, the positive environment created by success in the bargaining up to that point, and an enhanced level of trust.

This is not the type of packaging that occurs near the end of traditional negotiations that typically feature a mixed bag of genuine positions, and positions that were proposed as strategic give-aways. The latter are disguised throughout traditional negotiations so the package contains concessions on issues that the proposing party never expected to get. The main objective of traditional packages is compromise and concession. The main objective of IBB packaging is to achieve an interest-based settlement that addresses as many interests as possible.

The final stage of traditional negotiations is characterised by reluctant compromises and begrudging concessions. In contrast, the final stage of IBB is characterised by a willingness to yield, and a consensus attitude of acceptance as the best solution or settlement under the circumstances.

AN ILLUSTRATION OF THE IBB SEQUENCE AT WORK

An example may help the reader understand the IBB sequence better. In this example set in a privately run hospital, more nurses were applying through a central applications system for annual leave during peak periods than could be released by hospital management. This was leading to considerable friction in the workplace.

A ceiling on staffing levels and a policy of seniority in allocating annual leave were exacerbating the situation. On a number of occasions in the past, this issue had been sorted out with a temporary solution through adversarial bargaining, sometimes in the wake of industrial unrest and usually after local negotiations had failed and after a third party had been invited in to help the parties reach a settlement.

STEP ONE: FOCUSING THE ISSUE

Following some preparatory discussions the parties met to begin the interest-based bargaining or problem solving process. They stated the issue or problem to be resolved as: how can we amend the system of allocating annual leave such that more nurses can have holidays during peak periods and the hospital can provide an efficient and effective service?

During the focusing step the following aspects of the problem were highlighted:
- Many nurses couldn't get holidays when they wanted
- Some senior nurses got really long breaks while other nurses got none at the times they wanted them
- There were different seniority listings for holiday purposes in different units within the hospital
- Ceilings on staffing levels were exacerbating the problem
- Staff morale was being damaged by this problem
- Absenteeism was becoming a problem as nurses were going sick when leave was refused

Each bargaining team took away flip chart paper with the problem statement and with the points that emerged in the focusing session. They then identified their own interests and speculated a bit about the likely interests of the other party.

STEP TWO: THE INTERESTS

When the parties met to outline their interest to each other it emerged that the union's interest were:
- Members should within reason be able to take holidays when they want them
- There should be a fairer system for allocating annual leave
- The union wants to have a satisfied membership
- Improving staff morale
- Patient care
- Reducing absenteeism
- Adequate staffing levels
  After the union's interests had been discussed and clarified the management outlined their interests as being:
- Sustaining a high level of patient care
- Cost effectiveness: meeting budget targets and controlling staffing levels
- Having a leave allocation system that works for management and staff
- Good working relationships with staff and union
- Lower levels of absenteeism
- Adhering to health and safety standards
- Greater flexibility in terms of nurses being skilled to work in the different units

In the discussion of interests the union said that they understood why management were concerned about costs and budgets but that they did not fully share that interest. The management said they had a similar attitude towards the union's interest in having a satisfied membership. They both wanted to have a better/fairer system for allocating annual leave that worked to their mutual benefit. They both wanted to improve morale and reduce absenteeism. And they both had an interest around patient care.

The union said they shared the management interest around good working relationships between management, staff and the union although they had not come up with an interest along these lines themselves. They said the same thing for the health and safety interest. The management said they too wanted 'adequate' staffing levels but when it emerged that the union wanted additional staff employed the management said that that was not their understanding of 'adequate'.

In sum, they had identified a number of mutual interests (patient care, improving leave allocation system, reducing absenteeism, having good working relationships, adhering to health and safety standards, higher levels of staff satisfaction and morale), as well as some separate interests (satisfied union membership, cost effectiveness) and some conflicting ones (higher staffing levels and containing staffing levels).

STEP THREE: THE OPTIONS

Based on these mutual, separate and conflicting interests, the parties brainstormed the following options:
1. Joint review leading to agreed staffing levels
2. Consultant review of absenteeism and staff morale
3. Training to facilitate more flexible deployment between units
4. Ceiling on how much leave can be taken by one person during peak periods
5. Allocation of peak leave on rotation basis each year
6. Allocation of peak leave on a lottery basis each year
7. Allocation of peak leave to be on seniority but only up to two weeks at a time
8. Incentive of extra days for taking holidays outside peak periods
9. Incentive of money for taking holidays outside peak periods
10. Hospital to buy back leave not taken within certain limits each year
11. A single seniority listing for leave across the different units
12. Training for nurses to work in different units for periods each year
13. Change leave application system to allow nurses apply earlier in the year
14. Make application system more flexible so nurses can review their choices at some stage and not be stuck with them
15. Crèche facilities to be available during holiday peak periods to accommodate nurses opting to work during these periods

Without judging the options the parties noted that some options such as the suggested incentives were quite short-term while others such as the reviews and the provision of crèche facilities were probably more medium term.

STEP FOUR: THE STANDARDS

The parties decided to apply the three basic standards of feasible, beneficial and acceptable and to do this in a joint session. They noted that 'nothing was agreed until everything was agreed' and the nurses pointed out that they would have to consult their members on any tentative agreement. The managers said that if there were significant cost implications that they would have to go to the CEO for approval.

STEP FIVE: THE SETTLEMENT

Judging the options based on the standards, the parties utilised consensus decision-making to achieve a settlement that had four elements: a package of incentives aimed at encouraging nurses to take leave outside peak periods (this was strictly voluntary and agreed on a trial basis); a revised application system that kicked in earlier in the year to facilitate better planning; an agreement that there would be a ceiling on two weeks for leave taken during the peak periods; and a joint management-union review group to consider the seniority issue, the issue of training up nurses so that they could work in all units, and how the issues of morale and absenteeism might best be addressed.

CHAPTER SUMMARY

Interest-based bargaining follows a five-step sequence. Before the sequence commences there are important preparations for the parties to carry out. These include briefing constituents and getting a mandate to proceed from them. They also include forming bargaining or problem solving teams that have a reasonable size but more importantly have people with expertise and authority to make decisions. Joint training is crucial to effective IBB as are ground rules and facilitation.

The five steps follow this sequence: focusing the first issue to be handled; separately identifying interests around that issue and then sharing them in a joint session; using brainstorming to generate as many options as possible to satisfy as many interests as possible; deciding on agreed objective standards against which to measure the options; and then applying these standards to reach a settlement using consensus decision making.

In the next chapter we focus in detail on the tools and techniques used

The Interest-Based Bargaining Sequence

during the bargaining or problem solving sequence and we also address the role of facilitator before, during and after the bargaining or problem solving.

-6-

TOOLS, TECHNIQUES AND PROCESSES

'One of the most important challenges for negotiation facilitators is getting the parties to accept the possibility that, if they truly understand each other, their goals might not conflict'
Edgar Schein (1999), Process Consultation Revisited: Building the Helping Relationship.

'If the only tool you have is a hammer then every problem will look like a nail!'
Mark Twain.

INTRODUCTION

SUCCESSFUL INTEREST-BASED BARGAINING, as we have already seen, requires union and management participants to master new skills and techniques. If they fail to do so, they are likely to fall back on the skills and techniques they are familiar with from adversarial bargaining most of which are incompatible with IBB. This chapter describes in more detail the basic group process tools and techniques required by IBB. These are flip charting ideas, brainstorming ideas, and creating consensus based decisions. It is likely that many managers, union representatives and employees who are working in teams or partnership groups are already familiar with if not skilled in the use of the tools used in IBB. First of all, three other important aids to IBB are discussed: facilitation assistance, behavioural ground rules, and building trust.

FACILITATION

In traditional bargaining the parties negotiate directly without the involvement of a facilitator or other third-party. When they do ask a mediator to become involved, it is usually when they have reached an impasse or when talks have broken down. Interest-based bargaining, as already seen, is different in that the bargaining teams use a facilitator from the start. In both traditional adversarial and interest-based bargaining, it is essential that the facilitator or mediator behaves in a neutral manner and is seen at all time by the parties to be neutral.

In addition to neutrality, a facilitator in IBB should have experience in both IBB and in union-management relations. Facilitators who work mainly with groups other than management-union groups will not necessarily be tuned in to the distinctive features of management-union groups. On the other hand, facilitators with management-union experience will be familiar with traditional behaviours such as speaking through spokespersons, playing cards close to the chest, exploring issues through behind the scenes contacts, exaggerating positions etc. and will appreciate the difficulty that parties have in moving away from these behaviours.

These facilitators will recognise when traditional behaviours are beginning to surface and will know how to intervene effectively to protect the IBB process.

Many organisations already have 'partnership facilitators' who are well positioned to work with groups using IBB for the first time. As bargaining teams become more experienced and proficient at using interest-based methods, they may decide to dispense with the services of an external facilitator and to rotate the role of facilitator among themselves.

CORE VALUES OF FACILITATORS

For facilitators to be effective when working with groups they need to demonstrate independence and integrity so that a relationship of trust can be developed. Schwartz (1994) suggests that three core values should underpin the work of facilitators. These values seem to us to be very relevant in the management-union context. They are set out in Box 6.1:

BOX 6.1 CORE FACILITATION VALUES

Valid Information
- People share all relevant information
- People share in a way that others can understand
- People share in a way that others can validate.

Free and Informed Choice
- People define their own objectives and methods
- People are not manipulated or forced
- People base choices on valid information.

Internal Commitment to the Choice
- People feel personally responsible for their decisions
- People find their choices intrinsically compelling or satisfying.

The values around information sharing are entirely in keeping with the type of information sharing that needs to take place for IBB to be effective. It is not just a question of all the information being made available but information being available in a way that everyone can understand. What better way to provide for validation than through the joint gathering and analysis of data recommended in the IBB approach?

Also, the values around free and informed choice and avoiding manipulation and forcing fit with the voluntary nature of IBB and with the parties deciding not to use power. Finally, the values around internal commitment fit well with consensus decision making which leads to a sense of ownership of decisions made and of responsibility for 'living with' those decisions.

FACILITATION ROLES

The main roles of the facilitator at each step in the IBB sequence are summarized in Box 6.2 below. Typically before the bargaining starts, a facilitator will meet the parties to identify their expectations and assure all sides that they can establish a comfortable working relationship. To be effective the facilitator needs to have some awareness of the history of the bargaining group and of the main personalities on each side.

BOX 6.2 ROLE OF FACILITATOR IN INTEREST-BASED BARGAINING

Steps	Role of Facilitator
Before Bargaining Starts	• Meet parties to talk about upcoming bargaining • Facilitate information sessions/workshops for bargaining teams and constituents • Design and deliver training to bargaining teams • Help the parties to develop ground rules and a plan
During Bargaining Sequence in General	• Be a neutral process guide to the teams • Keep a record on the flip chart • Ensure ground rules are adhered to • Help to handle process difficulties • Help to strengthen relationships and skills • Clarify what is to happen at each step and how
Selecting and Focusing Issues	• Ask clarifying questions • Encourage teams to be concrete and specific • Keep teams away from suggesting solutions
Identifying Interests	• Facilitate discussion of interests • Help teams to clarify all the interests • Help teams to categorise interests • Steer teams away from arguments on interests
Developing Options	• Clarify rules and procedures of brainstorming • Facilitate and flip chart brainstorming session • Discourage evaluation of options at this stage
Creating Acceptable Standards	• Help teams to choose methods of evaluating options • Facilitate discussion and consensus around methods • Help teams to whittle down the number of options
Achieving Consensus or Settlement	• Help teams to apply agreed method to options • Check for consensus around chosen options • Facilitate discussion and agreement as to how final texts will be written and agreed
Writing Agreements	• Help, if requested, to draft texts for the teams
After Bargaining is Completed	• Help teams, if requested, to design information and decision making sessions for constituents • Help, if requested, to evaluate the process

The facilitator may then facilitate information and training workshops for the participants and their wider constituents. During the training or shortly afterwards the facilitator will help the group to develop ground rules and practical arrangements for the upcoming bargaining or problem solving sessions.

During the bargaining or problem solving sessions it will be the facilitator's role to be a neutral process guide to the bargaining teams. This will involve some practical work such as flip charting but more importantly it will involve observing the group in action and intervening to ensure that the ground rules are being adhered to. It will mean helping the group to address process difficulties such as straying away from the agreed process, helping with communications difficulties, helping if conflicts arise that the parties don't know how to handle effectively, protecting team members against attack etc. It will also be helpful if the facilitator keeps checking with the group that they are satisfied with the way things are going and that they are clear on the steps they have completed and the steps to come.

During the focusing session the facilitator may intervene with questions to help clarify and establish facts about the issue. The facilitator will, if necessary, advise the group not to stray either into interests or options.

The facilitator may offer to help parties when they are working separately at identifying their interests. Formulating interests, as we have seen already, is not easy for bargainers used to formulating positions. They may, therefore, welcome some assistance with this. It is not the role of a facilitator to suggest what their interests might be but it can be useful to ask questions that will help parties to identify and formulate their interests. It will also be helpful if the facilitator steers the group away from generating options during the separate and joint interests sessions.

When it comes to developing options using brainstorming the role of the facilitator will be critically important if the group is to avoid criticising and commenting on options as they are being called out. Also, if the group is slow in generating options the facilitator may need to encourage and challenge them to dig deeper and to be more energetic in their brainstorming. For example, where a group is mostly suggesting medium to long-term solutions the facilitator may challenge them to come up with some short-term answers or vice versa.

The facilitator will not, however, suggest any options, as this would be straying outside the bounds of neutrality. When all the options are listed it can seem daunting to groups, as we saw earlier, to make sense of them all. Again, the facilitator can help in the categorisation of options and in ordering them into a more manageable list for carrying forward to the next step.

Groups can get very bogged down at times in the discussion of standards or criteria for judging options. Sometimes they are keen to generate their own standards rather than using generic ones such as feasible, beneficial and acceptable. If so, the facilitator will have to facilitate a discussion around the proposed standards that ensures everyone has a say and that ensures there is common understanding around the meaning of whatever standards are adopted. The facilitator should probably encourage the group to consider the advantages and disadvantages of using the different approaches available before committing to any single approach.

In the application of the standards it will be helpful if the facilitator suggests a process or asks the group to suggest a process for this session. For example, will the parties take the options as listed on the charts or will they change the order of discussion to focus on the ones that seem to have the most potential for solving the problems? When options are rejected it may help if the facilitator asks is it possible to 'tweak' the option to make it work? Again, the more the facilitator encourages discussion around reasons for accepting and rejecting options the greater the likelihood of the teams amending options to make them work better for them.

Finally, when the formal bargaining or problem solving is completed the bargaining teams may ask the facilitator to assist in the writing up of documents and in the later evaluation of the bargaining process.

SPACE AND EQUIPMENT

Unlike traditional 'across the table' bargaining, IBB needs more space and more flexible furniture than a solid board room table for it to work effectively. An interest-based bargaining session, as will be clear from the descriptions so far, is more like a workshop than an adversarial bargaining session.

Participants will also need flip charts, paper, marking pens, tape or 'blue tack' (and walls suitable for 'posting' them) and furniture that can be moved around as small groups and separate caucus discussions take place.

GROUND RULES

As seen earlier, traditional adversarial bargaining occurs within some understood ground rules, albeit unwritten ones for the most part. Whether those ground rules are written or merely the result of habit, they should be examined and adjusted by unions and management if they intend to move from traditional to an interest-based approach. IBB ground rules must be consistent with the assumptions and practices of IBB.

Generally, ground rules fall into two categories: logistical and behavioural. The former involve practical matters like where to meet, starting date, starting time, rest breaks, availability of lunch etc.

Aligning the behavioural ground rules with IBB practices and assumptions is crucial to success. Some typical IBB behavioural ground rules are set out in Box 6.3.

BOX 6.3 SAMPLE IBB GROUND RULES

- No personal attacks or threats
- Treat everyone with respect
- Maximum openness, no hidden agendas
- Only one conversation and speaker at a time
- All agreements based on consensus
- No ownership of ideas by an individual or party, ownership only by the entire group
- No attribution of comments or ideas to named individuals
- Caucus breaks taken as necessary, but with due regard for potential negative impact on trust building and openness.
- Full and willing participation by all members
- Process concerns raised and dealt with when they occur
- Freedom to invent without criticism
- Probe links between interests and options respectfully
- Things said and done here will not be used later in adversarial bargaining
- Each session ends with a check on the need to 'sum up before we stand up'

In the main, these types of ground rules will be familiar to parties working together in teams or partnership groups. When the parties discuss and agree upon their ground rules, each member should understand the reasons for the rule and how it will be applied. This group and individual understanding of the ground rules will help the rules become self-enforcing. Thus each group member accepts his/her responsibility to follow the ground rules personally, but also to respectfully call attention to the failure of others to follow them.

TRUST BUILDING

Trust between union and management negotiators will, as we have seen in earlier chapters, make the IBB process much easier and more successful. But a high level of trust is not needed to start IBB because the IBB process itself builds trust based on the parties dealing honestly and transparently with each other. Many individuals participating in IBB for the first time report great surprise that their trust in the other side had grown as a result of the bargaining.

Unfortunately there is no simple or quick solution to building trust. It's a cliché but true that it takes a long time to build it but it can be destroyed in an instant. It can be useful for facilitators to raise this issue early on and to get the parties talking about what they mean by trust and what they expect of each other if they are to build trust.

It is important to tease out that trust is not a matter of each side making concessions to the other, as happens in adversarial bargaining. It can be helpful if the parties come to some understanding that trust is about doing what you say you will do and doing so all the time. Also, having some early warning arrangement that kicks in when either party for some reason cannot do what it has said it will do. When this happens, as it inevitably will for both management and trade unions, then the parties need to be upfront with each other at the earliest opportunity.

The development of trust should not be left to chance. A proactive effort is better. Here are several ideas that can help build trust:

- It is crucial that parties 'Walk the Talk', i.e. make it a practice to say what they intend to do and then do it exactly that way
- Behaving with transparency helps. This involves being clear, unambiguous, above board and open; and willing to create systems to assure commitments are being complied with.
- Looking for reasons or evidence in other's behaviour and words to trust them, instead of the opposite, is helpful.
- Acting and speaking the way you would like to see others acting and speaking will help to build trust.

A good facilitator will find teachable moments and exercises to help the group process their experience of growing trust. The combination of the group's willingness to allow, or better to encourage, trust to grow and the facilitator's skill in helping trust to grow will greatly enhance the parties trust level during the IBB process.

As discussed earlier, the practice of using caucuses or side meetings during bargaining is so typical of traditional negotiations that when used in IBB they could be harmful to trust. Therefore in IBB, their use should be kept to a minimum and be accompanied with some cautions.

FLIP CHARTING

The flip chart is an important tool that can be useful in all steps of IBB from selecting issues for bargaining through consensus decision making on the ultimate settlement. The recording on a flip chart may be done by the facilitator or by bargaining team members depending on circumstances.

When flip charting is done well, it helps focus everyone's attention on the matters being discussed and it provides a contemporaneous record of the bargaining. It can also help avoid situations where parties use their own notes to challenge statements or offers from the other side.

Often arrangements are made to have flip charts transcribed and copied between bargaining sessions. As the next bargaining session begins with a quick review of the prior session, each member will have a personal copy of the groups' bargaining notes from all previous sessions.

Since competent facilitators are skilled in flip chart usage, the facilitator should do the flip charting at the first several bargaining sessions. With the facilitator modelling best practices, group members will develop confidence in performing the charting later.

Recording on flip charts is not difficult but it does require some practice and following some basic guidelines. Here are some:

- Explain the use of the flip chart and get agreement for its use - mostly the use of flip charts is a routine matter but with some groups in some situations its use may be completely new and even controversial
- Check in advance that there is enough paper and good markers of different colours
- Display completed charts on the wall to help with reviewing
- Position flip chart stand where everyone can see it - if in doubt ask
- Stand sideways when writing and avoid giving your back to people
- Write clearly, using if possible block capitals rather than script, write large and legible words that can be seen from the farthest point in the room.

- Write on a level so that the texts don't run downwards or upwards
- If appropriate, divide the chart paper into columns, e.g. for/against, past/present or into rows, e.g. points one, two, three etc.
- If necessary repeat what someone has said to make sure you are accurately recording
- Where possible write exactly what someone has said and not an interpretation or a re-wording
- Don't slow things down by summarising or checking too much - the use of the flip chart should be unobtrusive
- Remember that authority belongs to the group, not to the chart writer. The chart writer is the group's tool
- Make sure that each chart has a clear heading, the day's date and is numbered in sequence for record keeping
- If the charted material is to be typed, help the typist understand what is expected.

BRAINSTORMING

Brainstorming is a technique used for generating lists of ideas, options, or solutions. Brainstorming is used to foster a creative approach to generating ideas by getting people to think beyond conventions and 'outside the box'. It can help stop a group from jumping to conclusions or from coming up with obvious answers or ones that may avoid difficult aspects of a problem.

It is not a technique for analysing or for decision-making; these happen later. Brainstorming has the advantage of putting all of a group's ideas on the table (or literally on a flip chart) for further discussion without immediate judgments on any particular ideas.

Brainstorming can be used to generate energy and to involve all group members in an activity but it does not work well late in a session or when people are very tired. The success of a brainstorming session depends on preparation and on following some simple rules. The main steps when doing brainstorming are:
- Introduce the session, and draw the participants' attention to the issue or problem statement the group is trying to address.

- Have the recorder write all responses on flipchart pages, and hang completed pages on the wall where participants can read them.
- Record responses as closely as possible to participants' own wording.

If a time limit is used, give a five-minute warning before time expires to allow everyone to contribute one last idea. Brainstorming rules are simple but important:

- All ideas, suggestions are welcome
- Withhold any judgments on suggestions; laughing, moaning, groaning and side comments sound like negative judgments to a speaker
- Encourage wild or novel suggestions
- Build suggestions on each other
- Go for quantity and not quality
- Treat everyone's suggestions equally.

The size of the two bargaining teams together should be small enough to allow effective brainstorming. Having ten to twelve participants in brainstorming is ideal. The composition of each team is important to getting the best results. Individuals with knowledge of the subject being discussed and with appropriate standing with those being represented in the bargaining are two key factors.

If circumstances require larger bargaining teams, some creativity will be required to do effective brainstorming. The size of the group can be reduced by: 1) excusing members who know little about the subject being discussed and who are willing to volunteer to step down for this exercise; and 2) using smaller working groups which work on a task before reporting back to the larger group.

A creative example was used in a Canadian situation in which bargaining was conducted by thirty-six negotiators speaking two languages. A 'fish-bowl' was created with eight chairs around a table and flip chart in the centre of the room where everyone else, sitting outside the fish-bowl could see and hear what was being said. Both team leaders designated three members to enter the fish-bowl. Two vacant chairs remained available for anyone outside the fish bowl to sit in long enough to offer their ideas before moving out again to the larger group.

Other variations on brainstorming include silent idea generation followed by the posting of these ideas on the wall or flip chart using index cards or 'post it' notes and the 'gallery method' where people post their ideas on separate charts and then walk around looking at each others' suggestions (like in a gallery), adding ideas where they choose to.

Where it seems to a facilitator that a few individuals are dominating the brainstorming then it is useful to use a 'round robin' technique, i.e. offer the opportunity to suggest an idea on a rotating basis one group member at a time. Any person who doesn't have an idea to offer when his/her turn comes up just says 'pass' and it becomes the next person's turn.

CONSENSUS DECISION MAKING

The primary method for making key decisions in IBB is consensus, not majority vote or allowing leaders to decide. Less important decisions, such as when and where to meet can be made by a vote or by the leaders. Decisions concerning which issues to discuss, the parties' interests, and selecting options are all so crucial in IBB that only consensus decisions will achieve IBB needs.

Two important results that consensus decisions achieve for IBB are protecting group members against majority decisions that are unpalatable to them and providing each group member with a sense of ownership in decisions and thereby causing them to live with the decision and defend it outside the group. The latter can be critically important when a decision involves advancing change within an organisation.

By way of definition, a group reaches consensus when all members agree upon a single course of action and when each member of the group can honestly say that:

- They believe their point of view has been heard and understood and that they understand everyone else's point of view, even if they do not agree with it,
- They support the course of action even though it may not be their first choice because it was decided upon fairly and openly and because it is the best solution for the group at this point in time.

Consensus decision making is not simply a matter of avoiding votes or leader's decisions. It is about the entire process of how the group surfaces and addresses difficulties and differences. It offers the group an opportunity to:

- Make the best use of the resources of each group member's knowledge, experience and opinion
- Reach high quality decisions, and
- Win the commitment of group members to support and implement the decision.

Reaching consensus involves articulating, understanding and discussing all relevant information and points of view before making an important decision.

The main elements of the consensus approach are:
- Listening actively to the views of others
- Encouraging different opinions to be expressed - treating differences as strengths
- Encouraging participation by all
- Sharing information as a resource for better decision making
- Not seeking agreement too quickly – speed is not always a virtue
- Not bargaining or trading support, rather deciding issues on their merits.

Even under the ideal circumstance of a good faith effort by skilled group members, consensus may not be reached on all issues. What happens then?

Often it helps to set the issue aside while addressing other issues. Success with other issues can restore the group's faith in their ability to achieve consensus. Or it may provide renewed determination to make con-sensus work. Also, inexperienced groups often conclude too soon that consensus has failed on a particular issue. Patience with each other and the process is needed in IBB. As in traditional bargaining, it is wise in IBB to select easier issues to deal with first, thus creating an early pattern of reaching consensus suc-cessfully.

A distinction was made earlier between integrative and distributive issues. Experience has shown that consensus can be achieved more easily with integrative issues. Distributive issues are more difficult primarily because they involve money and costs. In the next chapter, some tech-niques for handling distributive issues are discussed based on the U.S. experience with IBB.

CHAPTER SUMMARY

In this chapter we outlined the role of the facilitator whose main task is to be a process guide to the bargaining or problem solving teams. This means helping them to prepare through training and planning as well as through the elaboration of ground rules before the bargaining or problem solving starts. During the five steps there are a number of different supports that the facilitator can offer the bargaining teams. These include reminding them of their goals, their ground rules and the processes and techniques used in IBB. We also outlined a number of tools that have proven helpful in interest-based bargaining and problem solving. In the next chapter we turn to the U.S. experience of IBB over the past twenty-five years.

-7-

U.S. EXPERIENCE WITH IBB

'It appears that for most American unions and companies, the choices faced are either all-out conflict or all-out cooperation. The traditional way simply doesn't work well in highly competitive and volatile markets. Indeed, there is no option of maintaining or returning to the 'good old days' of traditional collective bargaining'.
    W.N. Cooke (1990): Labour Management Cooperation: New Partnerships or Going in Circles?

INTRODUCTION

THE HISTORY OF IBB in the U.S. extends back less than twenty-five years. The steady growth in IBB use in labour-management relations in the last 15 years stands in sharp contrast with an extremely adversarial and, in certain instances, violent history. In this chapter we set out that history and the recent flowering into IBB and labour-management partnerships. We also document what some of the key lessons have been about introducing and practicing interest-based bargaining approaches in the USA. We draw heavily on the experiences of the Federal Mediation and Conciliation Service, which has been training and facilitating IBB since the late 1980s, and which is without doubt the most significant repository of practical experience available.

BRIEF HISTORY OF U.S. COLLECTIVE BARGAINING

To understand the recent growth of IBB within U.S. collective bargaining, an understanding of the historic evolution of labour-management relations is necessary.
    Prior to World War One, the Courts had labelled trade unions as conspiracies in restraint of trade and had routinely issued injunctions prohibiting strikes. Neither custom nor legislation recognised any rights of workers or

unions. Since property rights were supreme, the police or the army violently enforced injunctions against unions and workers in the interest of protecting property. Where strikes occurred, they were frequently violent. The two industries most related to industrialisation, coal mining and railroading, provided dramatic evidence of hostility between industry and unionisation.

The war effort during 1917 to 1919 witnessed a major change in the fortunes of trade unions and collective bargaining. The tremendous growth in war related production and the need for uninterrupted war products resulted in forced cooperation between labour and management. With the government acting as the enforcer, trade unions were allowed to form and negotiate collective bargaining agreements. Government mediation services and wartime agencies responsible for production helped diminish strikes to near zero while union membership soared to unheard of levels. Collective bargaining agreements became common-

place in the war industry. One million union members in 1900 grew to 5 million during the war.

Early forms of union-management cooperation emerged during World War One in the shape of 'shop committees' comprised of equal numbers of representatives of both employees and management to help ensure industrial peace and full production (Cohen-Rosenthal and Burton, 1997).

When World War One ended, employers successfully returned labour management relations to pre-war conditions. The slow down of the economy as it adjusted to peacetime allowed employers to cut wages and refuse to renew collective bargaining agreements. Ironically, the enormous number of strikes that followed played well with an employer strategy of depicting unions as foreign, socialistic and anti-American. Union membership declined throughout the 1920s, never reaching the wartime high until the New Deal legislation in the 1930s.

THE NEW DEAL LABOUR LAW

Legislative and administrative actions in the 1930s ushered in a growth in union membership and collective bargaining that dwarfed the war boom. New legislation limited the use of injunctions against unions, provided for employee elections to select union representation for collective bargaining, and limited management activities aimed at interfering with union activities and collective bargaining (Kochan et al, 1994). The resulting membership growth was remarkable. By 1935 membership stood at 3.5 million or 13% of the work force and by 1940 membership reached 9 million or 27%. The use of mediation grew with the expansion of collective bargaining.

During World War Two, union membership and collective bargaining continued to expand with production requirements greatly exceeding the demand of World War One. By the war's end, union membership reached an all time high of 40 million or 35% of the workforce. The growth of collective bargaining, accompanied by amazingly few strikes, was aided by an expanded mediation service and an aggressive War Labour Board that decided collective bargaining issues when parties reached impasse. One of the War Labour Board's biggest impact decisions required labour agreements to include a provision for arbitration of grievances. This practice became universal following the war, and earned further support in 1960 when the Supreme Court ordered Federal Courts to limit their actions in the area of collective bargaining to enforcing agreements to arbitrate and arbitration awards.

When World War Two ended, the transition to a peacetime economy was difficult. The year following the war saw more major strikes occur than any time before or since in U.S. history. During the winter and spring of 1945-46, five major industries were on strike at the same time, with five million workers idle in steel, auto, meatpacking, coal and electrical manufacturing.

President Truman, like Wilson had in 1920, called a White House conference of top labour and management representatives to seek some accommodation in the public interest. Truman's conference produced modest results with an agreement recommending improvements to the government's mediation service.

NEW LABOUR LAW

The following spring a newly elected Republican Congress enacted a major legislative amendment which created a new mediation service, the Federal Mediation and Conciliation Service, prohibited some union activities, and provided a process for dealing with national emergency disputes. Fear of foreign ideas was again used against unions with a provision requiring all union officials to sign non-communist affidavits as a pre-requisite to using the labour law. A few years later, Congress recognised the absurdity of the provision and removed it.

The new labour law promised to oversee collective bargaining even-handedly between labour and management. The calm, good times of the 1950s provided a period for labour and management to work out relation-ships and useful practices to implement the new law in ways that served their separate interests. The practices and patterns that evolved in the 1950s would hold reasonably well until the 1980s.

The ever-rising U.S. economy allowed unions to demand improvements in working conditions, wages and benefits. Management resisted union demands, but ultimately, over a thirty-year period, they conceded many improvements. These included benefits unheard of earlier such as holidays and sick leave, health and life insurance, premium pay for night and week-end work, rest breaks, paid lunch periods, to name just a few. The rising economy allowed management to pass the employment costs on to their customers, just as their competitors were able to do.

Collective bargaining in the public sector grew dramatically in the 1960s and early 1970s with many states passing statutes supporting the right of public sector employees to join unions and engage in collective bargaining (Brock and Lipsky, 2003).

Collective bargaining from the 1950s to the 1980s was strongly tradition-al and adversarial, since both sides possessed nearly equal skills and the strength to push the other side. They were well-balanced adversaries. During earlier periods, they bargained in an adversarial way, but not as equals.

During the two world wars and following the new labour law in the 1930s, unions experienced greater power with government help. During other periods, management benefited from the strong commitment of the Courts to private property rights and the enforcement power of the police.

NEW PARADIGM

New circumstances arriving in the 1980s significantly altered the balance of power. Foreign competition started to pinch the U.S. economy as its tech-nological and productivity advantages were eroded by foreign advance-ments. As management lost the ability to pass labour costs on to cus-tomers, labour costs were identified as the villain. When the pro-business Reagan Administration came to power in the early 1980s, a paradigm shift occurred.

The Administration began with a tough period of economic recession that drove up unemployment and created uncertainty. Next an ill-advised strike by air traffic controllers provided Reagan the opportunity to fire and replace thousands of strikers. This dramatic and unprecedented move by Reagan, a former head of the actors' union, won praise from the travelling public and the business community. But more importantly, it depicted unions as a selfish interest group that had become too strong, as the problem and not part of the solution to regaining the nation's competitive edge. Practices that had been outside the norm for forty years became legitimate. If the President could replace strikers, why shouldn't corporations aggressively take on unions in their drive to restore the nation's competitive advantage?

Thus the 1980s saw an attack on hard-won union gains and a significant decline in union membership. Unionised plants were closed, labour agreements saw wage and benefit reductions, strikes were lost before starting, and bargaining featured union concessions in a hope of achieving job security in the face of massive lay-offs. Adding to union troubles, Reagan appointees to the National Labour Relations Board shifted collective bargaining rules to significantly favour management in a rush to support free enterprise over anything else. During the 1980s, union membership declined from 23% to 16% of the workforce, from 20 to 16 million. As this decline continued during the 1990s, staff reductions and services declined, forcing union mergers and a defensive union mentality.

U.S. IBB HISTORY

The use of IBB in labour-management relations, under a variety of names, began to appear in the late 1980s after remaining only a textbook theory since the late 1960s. As concerns about the impact of foreign competition began to emerge, private sector organisations began to follow two distinct approaches to labour-management relations. One approach sought to operate in a 'union free environment' by aggressively negotiating or 'forcing' deep reductions in wages and benefits, and 'escaping' labour-management relationships by closing unionised plants and opening new plants in anti-union locations. The other approach, a 'fostering' one, sought to establish more cooperation with unionised work forces, even to the extent of limited labour-management partnerships.

During the 1980s, trade unions could not resist wage and benefit cuts and layoffs, as their membership and finances declined. These new circumstances challenged traditional union approaches to labour-management relations, and forced them to respond, at first reluctantly, but gradually more willingly, to the cooperative initiatives proposed by some employers.

It seems unlikely that unions would have shifted to IBB if traditional bargaining had continued to produce the results it did from the end of World War Two until the end of the 1970s. That period of phenomenal growth in wages and an expanding list of new benefits resulted from a traditional negotiation process that had served unions and their members very well. But for foreign competition that ended those golden years, traditional bargaining might still be king.

While it can be argued that IBB should be used simply because it is a more enlightened way to negotiate, the fact is that for most unions IBB is not their first choice. Given different circumstances, most unions would be pleased to be fighting the good fight for their members using traditional adversarial bargaining.

It is not surprising that it took the presence of powerful external pressures for trade unions to contemplate radical alternatives to adversarial bargaining since it is commonly assumed that it takes a powerful stimulus or 'felt need' for people in organisations to accept significant changes generally. Not all cases, however, grew from immediate crisis. Some of the exemplar cases, Shell Sarnia and Saturn Corporation for example, were planned and developed over a period of years (Heckscher, 1996; Woodworth and Meek, 1995; Rubinstein and Kochan, 2001).

There are also some unions that now actively promote the adoption of interest-based bargaining and other cooperative approaches to labour-management relationships. The rationale for such a policy is that unions' interests need to extend beyond pay and conditions to include the critical decisions that affect workers' security and wages such as company strategy, allocation of resources, workplace organisation, the use of technology and other decisions about quality and productivity (Lazes and Savage, 1997).

While labour-management relations had always been adversarial, there also had been cooperative exceptions. Cooperation occurred during both world wars and the Korean War. Joint committees supporting safety had been widely used for many years. On the other hand, the labour management conferences following both world wars, which were called to address labour-management relations as a national issue, turned out to be very poor harbingers for cooperation (Kochan et al, 1986).

The 1980s movement toward greater cooperation (Kochan et al, 1984) drew assistance from the Labour Department's creation of a Bureau of Labour-Management and Cooperative Programmes. The Bureau advised labour and management on ways to establish cooperative efforts. The Bureau's work included training and orientation programmes, publications, studies, videos and consulting. Also the Bureau's two-day organisation development programme called Partners in Change (PIC) was widely used as a joint experience for labour and management in moving their relationship to a cooperative future. The development of PIC was a joint effort of the Bureau and FMCS.

Recognising that collective bargaining, with over a half century of history, constituted the most adversarial and least cooperative segment of labour-management relations, the Bureau initially focused its efforts on labour-management activities outside of collective bargaining. As a result, a bifurcated relationship was encouraged between the parties' cooperative, day-to-day relationship and their periodic, adversarial collective bargaining negotiations.

The 1981 book *Getting to Yes* popularised an interest-based approach to problem solving and negotiations that provided a useful alternative to power based negotiations, an alternative that had remained largely theoretical since Walton and McKersie's 1965 book, *A Behavioural Theory of Labour Negotiations*. While the impact of *Getting to Yes* began to catch on in other conflict arenas, it held little to no sway in collective bargaining during most of the 1980s.

Late in that decade, the U.S. author of this volume developed a two-day IBB training programme and tested it with labour-management pairs identified by FMCS. Following the training, parties willing to try IBB in their negotiations were given help in getting started. Large numbers of FMCS mediators received training in the use of interest-based bargaining. Initially, IBB seemed to be more compatible with school teachers and other public employees, and parties without a long history in traditional bargaining. By the mid-1990s, however, a growing number of private sector employers were using IBB.

With FMCS leading the way, IBB training and use soon exceeded everyone's expectations. A large boost to the use of IBB came in 1993 when President Clinton issued an Executive Order directing Federal Agencies to create partnerships with the unions of their employees and to engage them in IBB. The incidence of partnerships and IBB increased throughout the 1990s, and by the advent of the Bush Administration, the use of IBB in Federal Government was significant. President Bush, however, cancelled the Clinton Executive Order. While that cancellation did not make partnering or using IBB illegal, Bush appointees who headed agencies discouraged their use.

IBB IN THE USA TODAY

Recent surveys show that there is considerable awareness and use of interest-based bargaining among labour and management negotiators in the U.S. today (Cutcher-Gershenfeld and Kochan, 2004). About eight out of ten union negotiators said they were familiar with IBB and slightly less than six out of ten said they had used IBB. Among management respondents, slightly less than seven out of ten said they were familiar with IBB and slightly less than six out of ten said they had used it.

Of the management and union negotiators who said that they had used IBB, about one third of them said that they had engaged in some joint training, less than a quarter said that they provided advance notice to their constituents that they were using this approach, and about one in five said they used joint sub-committees or task forces. During the bargaining process there was extensive use of brainstorming and over two-thirds reported using consensus decision making. On the other hand, there was limited use of facilitators.

More than half of the parties familiar with IBB reported an increase in the use of brainstorming as negotiations moved to a conclusion but a similarly large number reported a move to traditional bargaining as negotiations moved to a conclusion. This suggests that some bargaining teams are using a completely interest-based process while others are combining elements of IBB with more traditional adversarial approaches. Later we will describe an approach to bargaining developed by the FMCS called 'modified traditional bargaining', which is a hybrid form of bargaining using elements of both interest based and adversarial approaches.

Perhaps the highest profile example of the use of IBB in the U.S. today is the Kaiser Permanente case, which we now discuss in outline.

IBB IN KAISER PERMANENTE

Kaiser Permanente (KP) is the leading not-for-profit health maintenance organisation, serving 8.6 million members in 18 states in the U.S. Fully 80 per cent of its operations are in California where it was founded in 1933. In 1997 KP and a coalition of 26 unions representing some 57,000 employees created what is now the largest partnership in the U.S. (McKersie et al, 2004). This partnership was a response to severe competitive pressures from for-profit health care providers which had led to strained relations and disputes around cost reductions, redundancies and other changes aimed at making KP more efficient and effective.

In 2000 the parties negotiated their first major contract under the new partnership agreement. They designed and implemented the largest and most complex set of interest-based negotiations carried out in the field of industrial relations. Traditionally, contract bargaining had involved separate negotiations involving more than thirty different unions. Between March and October 2000 the parties reached a five-year national agreement on all their contract issues affecting the membership of the 26 unions concerned.

Box 7.1 gives the briefest summary of the interest-based negotiation process, to use the KP term, used by the parties to reach this agreement.

BOX 7.1 INTEREST BASED NEGOTIATION IN KAISER PERMANENTE

All of the representatives received a three-day training programme in interest-based principles and problem solving. There was a Common Issues Committee (CIC) to oversee and co-ordinate the bargaining. There were parallel national and local negotiations taking place within an agreed framework.

The central bargaining agenda was divided into seven areas: wages, benefits, work-life balance, performance and workforce development, quality and service, employee health and safety, and work organization. Each area was allocated to a national Bargaining Task Group (BTG). These groups comprised of traditional bargaining representatives but, for the first time, they also included operational managers with expertise in the areas concerned. Each BTG engaged in an interest-based process of joint study, problem solving and negotiations using guidelines provided by the CIC. Each BTG had the services of two facilitators. The groups met for a few days every other week and between times the members consulted with constituents. The outcomes of the BTG process were ratified by the CIC and these then provided parameters for the local bargaining.

The bargaining process had five steps: 1) defining the problem; 2) determining interests; 3) developing options, often using brainstorming; 4) agreeing on criteria for choosing options; and 5) selecting a solution.

In the local bargaining the parties opened by identifying issues they wanted to see resolved. Issues were then assigned to sub-groups that met once a week for about twelve hours at a time. All of the groups had facilitators to help them.

At the critical stage of focusing on agreement the parties agreed to identify 'make or break' items that had to be resolved before agreement could be reached. This was seen as a realistic approach. Also, given the size of the operation both sides found it necessary to have more caucus meetings than would normally be advised. Not all issues were resolved locally or through the BTGs and in the case of wages the settlement emerged at CIC level.

Source: Kaiser Permanente: Using Interest Based Negotiations to Craft a New Collective Bargaining Agreement (McKersie et al, 2004).

The negotiations involved nearly 400 union and management representatives and more than 20 neutral facilitators, mostly from FMCS but including some from a private consulting firm. An important ground rule that was never used was that both sides had the option of pulling out of the process at any time. These contract negotiations have been described as the signal accomplishment of the KP partnership to date and as one of the most significant breakthrough negotiations in U.S. labour relations in recent times (McKersie et al, 2004).

FMCS AND IBB

In the past ten years, IBB became a mainstay of the FMCS mediators' workload, encompassing joint IBB training and facilitation of IBB negotiations. Later as IBB had taken hold in FMCS, mediators began using it to help resolve grievances and to break impasses in collective bargaining negotiations. Even more recently, FMCS mediators began to struggle with the difficulties in using IBB on distributive issues. We discuss each of these topics in turn.

IBB TRAINING

The FMCS training in IBB is typically two days in length and is conducted jointly with labour and management. Like training discussed earlier in this volume, it uses interactive exercises that engage participants in experiencing IBB in contrast with their adversarial bargaining experience. An IBB model is presented and an opportunity to get-a-feel-for the process is provided.

By the conclusion of the training, participants have the capacity to determine if they are willing to undertake IBB with the other side, having had some experience of trying out the new approach with them in the training.

At the conclusion of the training, the participants are told about facilitation and the sound reasons for using it in their negotiation to avoid slipping back into traditional behaviours and jinxing the effort. Most participants agree to try IBB and at least start their bargaining with FMCS facilitation assistance. Most FMCS mediators will not work with bargaining teams wishing to use IBB but unwilling to take joint training.

IBB FACILITATION

While mediation and facilitation have similarities, they have differences as well. Since mediators are settlers they get directly involved in the content of negotiations and their role is to help parties reach agreements by suggesting possible solutions to them separately and jointly. When mediators sense that a settlement is possible, they act to achieve it. That highly developed skill is what makes a good mediator.

Facilitators, on the other hand, get much less involved, if at all, in the content of negotiations. As we saw earlier, their role is essentially that of process expert and guide. For a mediator to facilitate IBB, restraint is required, so the IBB process can play out fully without the involvement of the facilitator in the content of the negotiations or problem solving. The IBB facilitator assists the parties to use the IBB process to settle their issues.

FMCS mediators are trained to mediate and facilitate. They have the know-how and skill to switch to whichever third party process is appropriate in the circumstance they face. Typically when IBB is being used, facilitation is the preferred third party assistance needed.

Here is a real life experience that contrasts the two. In the early 1990s before many FMCS mediators were conversant with IBB, the author had trained the union and management representatives at a plant in the Mid West in how to use IBB. The local FMCS mediator asked if he could attend the bargaining, which the US author was facilitating, and that was agreed.

At the lunch break on the second day, the FMCS mediator spent some time talking first with the lead representative of one side and then the other. Before bargaining resumed following lunch, the mediator told the US author that he had talked with the two representatives about a settlement he had mediated recently on the same issue the parties were now bargaining. He said that he was confident that he could persuade them to agree to that same settlement.

The author told him that since the parties had settled several issues already using IBB and were making good progress on the current issue, he should not circumvent the IBB process for a quicker settlement. On that assumption the bargaining resumed in the afternoon. The FMCS mediator, however, continued talking privately to the lead negotiators when opportunities arose to broker a settlement.

To resolve the matter, the U.S. author eventually arranged a meeting with the two lead negotiators and the FMCS mediator to clarify the seperate roles of mediator and facilitator. The lead negotiators opted to continue the IBB process and the mediator accepted that attempts to mediate in a traditional manner had not been helpful to the IBB process.

GRIEVANCE MEDIATION AND IBB

In recent years, FMCS has been emphasising its grievance mediation services. In the U.S. context, a grievance is an alleged violation of the labour agreement, for example: firing or disciplining an employee, failing to pay benefits due, failing to follow other requirements in the parties' labour agreement. At least 95% of U.S. labour agreements contain a grievance procedure, which is a series of steps up through higher levels of authority representing both labour and management. Typically, the process terminates in final and binding arbitration. Because of complaints of the slowness, cost, adversarial nature and win/lose outcomes associated with arbitration, some parties have inserted a mediation step in their grievance procedure just prior to arbitration.

In recent years, FMCS mediators have been mediating grievances under such a provision. Since the parties view grievances as matters to dispose of so they can get on with their work, grievance mediation is primarily a problem solving process. Mediators comfortable with IBB find it effective to introduce the parties to IBB as a convenient and efficient problem solving process. If the parties are familiar with IBB, the process is easiest. If they are not, the mediator engages them in an on-the-spot tutorial on IBB and asks them to try the process. Typically the parties see using IBB as a low risk exercise on an issue that they have failed to resolve in negotiation during prior steps of the grievance procedure.

A successful resolution of a grievance using IBB provides the mediator with the opportunity to suggest joint training for grievance handlers. If the parties' next round of collective bargaining is on the horizon, the mediator might use their successful use of IBB to suggest using IBB in their up-coming negotiations.

BREAKING COLLECTIVE BARGAINING IMPASSES

Mediators often get involved in collective bargaining negotiations when the parties have reached an impasse and are unable to move ahead. For most mediators, this is an exciting and challenging juncture in their work. It is a point when the parties are feeling disappointed and frustrated, and probably angry at each other. Therefore, the parties are looking to the mediator to work his/her magic, to lead them to a resolution that has eluded them. Mediators have tools and techniques that they traditionally use to assist the parties - persuade, challenge, suggest, proposal, caucus, etc. - all of which are linked to and compatible with traditional bargaining. With the advent of IBB, mediators have a new tool.

It is likely such parties have not been exposed to IBB. Here is how the mediator might proceed after being briefed by the parties on the issues causing their impasse: 1) the mediator tells the parties he/she does not want to know their positions on the unresolved issues; 2) the mediator explains that he/she wants to help them work on the first issue using an approach different from what they have been using; 3) if they express any reservations, he/she will explain that he/she has had success using this process to resolve impasses, and wants them to at least give it a try; 4) the mediator explains the difference between a position and an interest; 5) using a flip chart to help them through the IBB steps, the mediator begins with their interests on the first issue

When IBB succeeds in helping the parties overcome their impasse and achieve settlement, the mediator can discuss the process they have just used and suggest that some training would enhance their skills in grievance handling and in their next collective bargaining round.

USING IBB ON DISTRIBUTIVE ISSUES

Earlier a distinction was made between integrative bargaining issues and distributive bargaining issues. The latter involves costs and resources, and generally involves issues likely to lead to one party winning at the other party's expense. Or said another way: what one party gains, the other must give up. While all parties have found distributive bargaining difficult, many have found ways to make IBB work even on these issues. However, some parties have used IBB for all their integrative issues, and have then shifted to traditional bargaining to address their distributive issues, believing that IBB cannot achieve resolution.

U.S. Experience with IBB

Because of these difficulties with IBB and distributive issues, FMCS asked its mediators, who have discovered ways of helping IBB deal with distributive issues, to share their ideas in writing (FMCS, 2004). Forty FMCS mediators have written short papers on their experiences. Most of their writings reflect how significantly collective bargaining has been impacted by the paradigm shift of the 1980s. To a greater or lesser extent, bargaining is now focused within the limits or parameters that the product or service market of the employer imposes. Those limits or parameters constitute the 'pot of money' available for bargaining, in effect, the 'bottom line.' How precisely those limits or parameters are iden-

tified, i.e. from just a sense of the limits to precision beyond a reasonable doubt, is determined by the parties' preference and the availability and reliability of information.

Suggested methods for gathering parameter-focused information vary from extensive research by joint committees to a mere presentation by the employer on the financial status of the business and industry. Falling between those extremes are arrangements for the employer to provide information on any question raised by the union, to jointly gathering information on several agreed upon comparable employers.

Once information has been gathered, shared, understood and acknowledged, the negotiators turn to how the available funds will be allocated as between wages and health care, for example. Some attention also might be devoted to ways to increase the amount of money available, in effect expanding the 'pot of money' or pie, through productivity improvements or cost savings ideas, for example.

A few of the mediators did not use data gathering of any kind to help IBB work through the distributive issues. For example, one approach was for the parties to take each distributive issue, one at a time, through the first three IBB steps, while allowing as many caucuses as the parties wanted. Once all issues had been through the three steps, the parties held caucus meetings to prepare a package settlement created from the options developed on all the issues. Then the parties presented their package settlement to the other side in a joint session. As they discussed possible solutions, they applied their standards and discussed interests. While the mediators report that the process was slow, they found it effective in reaching a consensus solution on all the distributive issues.

Several mediators also wrote about very creative ways of handling distributive issues. One example moved each distributive issue through the steps to a consensus on their best 'possible options', with the negotiators agreeing to behave during this phase of bargaining 'as if money were no object.' This remarkable condition, the mediator wrote, allowed the parties to focus on the issue and the best possible solution. Once such a solution is arrived at on each issue, an agreed upon cost is assigned to each. Then the parties discuss ways in which they could modify their best possible solution to fit within the overall cost of all distributive issues.

Several mediators wrote about using the FMCS TAGS (Technological Assisted Group Solutions) programme to aid IBB with all issues. TAGS is a network of Internet servers, mobile computers, electronic conferencing facilities and customised software, which FMCS has used to assist labour and management conduct more effective and efficient meetings. TAGS allows groups to brainstorm and reach consensus anonymously at individual keyboards from several geographic locations.

Most mediators acknowledge the usefulness of the parties' successful experiences during integrative IBB. Carrying positive feelings into distributive IBB is extremely important, even though the exact same process and steps may not be used. Some mediators wrote of helping parties assess their earlier experience, and discussing the need to carry them forward with some adjustments into handling a distributive agenda through interest-based bargaining.

A few mediators wrote of the need for additional ground rules to cover distributive IBB, including a process for gathering information, early listing of distributive issues, early discussion of those issues while staying focused on interests and not positions, the relationship of trust building to sharing honest data, steps to be used, and continuing need for facilitation.

MODIFIED TRADITIONAL BARGAINING

Modified traditional bargaining (MTB) is a hybrid form of bargaining that FMCS developed for bargaining teams that did not want to use adversarial bargaining fully and that did not want to change over either to a complete interest-based approach (FMCS, 2002). This form of bargaining, it is argued, is suitable for a large population of bargaining teams that fall between those comfortable with traditional bargaining and those comfortable with IBB, i.e. bargaining relationships desiring and capable of some level of cooperation but without a process to employ.

MTB, simply defined, is a process aimed at allowing parties interested in cooperation to maximise the cooperative potential in bargained issues. It is a process midway between traditional bargaining and IBB in terms of cooperation.

The types of bargaining teams likely to be interested in MTB might be early on the path to a collaborative relationship and seeking to increase their level of cooperation at the bargaining table. Or they might want to cooperate but recognise that they face some clearly divisive issues that don't lend themselves to a cooperative resolution. Or they may be faced with a business environment simultaneously forcing cooperation for survival but limiting it at the same time. MTB, then, is for those groups seeking to cooperate at the bargaining table but unlikely to reach full consensus on every issue.

MTB is based on the premise that levels of ability to cooperate vary and that the range of issues being brought to the bargaining table are likely to include some with a high potential for integrative solutions as well as some with little potential for such outcomes. Like IBB, MTB requires joint training and is conducted in a structured way with the help of a facilitator. It provides for fully exploring issues and maximising interest attainment. In so doing, it accomplishes an improvement in the relationship as a byproduct.

Generally, the starting point for FMCS in working with a group that is interested in MTB is a group presentation that outlines the fundamental expectations, helpful guidelines, steps, and techniques that are necessary to effectively use the process. Of particular importance is the ability of the participants to accept the underlying expectations and guidelines. Since behaviour is driven by expectations and adherence to guidelines, participants have an early test of their possible success in using the MTB process. An inability to embrace the expectations and guidelines of MTB will translate into an inability to successfully follow the steps and use the techniques.

FMCS also advises that parties considering the use of MTB should consider if they could meet the following requirements before embarking on its use:

- Some evidence of commitment to developing a cooperative relationship.
- The willingness of the parties to share important bargaining information.
- Sufficient time to complete the sequence of decision making, training, and application of the process.
- A willingness to forego use of power as a first choice to secure outcomes.

• An understanding and acceptance of the process by constituents.

The MTB steps have three distinct phases, into which issues are grouped by distinctive characteristics. The first phase deals with non-economic issues believed to have a high potential for cooperation. The second phase deals with non-economic issues believed to have low potential for cooperation and the third phase deals with economic issues.

In phase one each issue is worked through the following five steps: focus the selected issue, share interests, generate options, hold a resolution discussion, and reach tentative agreement or place the issue in a 'holding bin' or 'parking lot' for later discussion if it is not resolved.

The phase two steps are: focus the selected issues one at a time and share interests on each of these, then develop positions on the phase two issues and the phase one issues in the 'holding bin', then exchange positions; then negotiate around these positions.

The phase three steps are: economic information presentations, sharing of interests, development of positions, exchange of positions, and negotiation around these positions.

As well as using flip charting, brainstorming and ground rules, the parties also use a tool called 'binning' which is the placing of unresolved issues into a temporary 'parking lot' after exhausting the possibilities of a cooperative resolution. This postpones the taking of positions until the appropriate place in the process.

The importance of following the sequence is two-fold. First, it lays out a natural problem solving sequence. Second, it assists all of the participants in staying on the MTB track and not shortchanging problem solving efforts.

MTB differs from adversarial bargaining in that the parties begin with a discussion of interests around the selected issues and they attempt to brainstorm solutions, and it differs from IBB in that the parties prepare positions around issues on which they have not succeeded in reaching a consensus settlement.

IBB, CO-OPERATION AND PARTNERSHIP

In the U.S. the words 'cooperation' and 'partnership' have often been used interchangeably. For many, partnership is a more advanced stage of cooperation. There are many examples of cooperation that do not constitute a partnership. For parties whose relationships have been adversarial, cooperative efforts tend to begin tentatively and hesitantly (as, indeed, they also do in Ireland), with labour and management both awaiting proof of the other side's intentions and trustworthiness, before committing themselves to the handling of significant issues through cooperative mechanisms.

As seen earlier, the 1980s paradigm shift began in reaction to foreign competition and various reactions set in among labour and management, including anger, confusion and distress. For some labour-management pairs, the thought began to emerge that while they had identified each other as the enemy, in fact their enemy was low cost, high productivity competitors. As they looked to these competitors, they learned about QWL (quality of working life) programmes, Quality Circles, and other forms of working together (Kochan et al, 1984).

Those U.S. firms that attempted these working-together efforts gained productivity improvements and competitiveness (Kochan and Osterman, 1994). As they examined other aspects of their relationship such as grievance handling and collective bargaining, labour and management recognised that IBB could transform those remaining conflictive areas of their relationship.

Thus IBB is supplemental to both cooperative efforts and partnerships. Indeed, it has been argued in the U.S. that interest-based bargaining thrives best within the context of a labour-management partnership (Fonstad et al, 2004).

SUMMARY

The U.S. has a long collective bargaining history that influenced how labour and management came to use IBB. The U.S. has a longer history with IBB than Ireland. Certainly there are large differences between the two countries in terms of size, diversity and the complexity of their labour relations systems. But there are similarities as well, especially around traditional approaches to labour-management relations and to traditional adversarial bargaining. There are also similarities between partnership initiatives at workplace level in the U.S. and Ireland. Certainly, the overriding reason for using IBB animates both countries as they deal with the hard realities of foreign competition while endeavouring to maintain a reasonable standard of living for citizens.

The history of IBB in the U.S. shows clearly that the process can be used, not always without difficulty needless to say, to resolve major and complex issues relating to the pay and conditions of large numbers of employees. The history also shows that it can be used effectively to resolve individual grievances and to break impasses in traditional adversarial bargaining. It shows that IBB is evolving and changing as parties become more experienced in its use and as the demands placed on it become greater, bearing out the old saying that 'where there's a will, there's a way'.

-8-

CONCLUSION

'Change and innovation in the workplace will play a pivotal role in determining our capacity to develop as a dynamic, inclusive, knowledge-based economy and society. What takes place within the workplace is central to the capacity to innovate and adapt to change – for the Irish economy as a whole as well as for individual organizations.'
Report of the Forum on the Workplace of the Future (NCPP, 2005).

INTRODUCTION

IN THIS SHORT CHAPTER we summarise the key points that we made in the earlier chapters. We summarise what we think can be stated with reasonable certainty about interest-based bargaining or problem solving in the light of the American and Irish experiences. We look at the factors that are conducive to adoption of interest-based bargaining. Finally, we speculate about the prospects for the wider adoption of IBB in Irish workplaces.

KEY POINTS

In essence, we have argued that in Ireland the dominant position of adversarial collective bargaining as the principal means of communication and engagement between managers, trade union representatives and employees in unionised workplaces has been eroded in recent years. This erosion can be explained by a number of inter-connected factors. These are:
- A market-driven shift in emphasis in industrial relations away from trade union concerns with pay and conditions towards management concerns around organisational change and improvement
- The national sponsorship by government, employers and trade unions of new channels of communication and engagement for managers, employees and union representatives, frequently badged as 'partnership'

- A preference among managers for avoiding the handling of many workplace issues through adversarial bargaining and for the direct involvement of employees in workplace issues
- A desire among employees and union representatives to have more of a say in how decisions are made about workplace issues
- The removal of pay bargaining in most instances from the workplace to national level
- The removal of many conditions of employment from the workplace bargaining agenda into legislation-based third-party procedures.
- The increasing awareness and use of joint problem solving tools in the workplace

Taken together, these factors have created opportunities in many unionised organisations for managers, union representatives and employees to work together using more cooperative methods such as open dialogue leading to consensus, joint problem solving, and most recently interest-based bargaining.

There are, as acknowledged earlier, many organisations in which this is not happening and in which the decline of collective bargaining is probably leading to stronger managerial control over the workplace agenda and to a reduction in union influence. Indeed, as one observer has commented, there are many situations where even adversarial relations are no longer available to trade unions (Cooke, 1990). Our focus, however, is on those organisations likely to be developing more cooperative approaches.

It may also happen that the changing composition of the workforce and the trade union movement away from a traditional male, 'blue collar', private sector orientation towards a female, 'white collar' or professional and public service orientation will strengthen the trend towards the use of more cooperative approaches to dispute resolution and problem solving (Kolb and Williams, 2000; NCPP, 2005; LRC, 2005).

On this basis, we have argued that IBB is an idea 'whose time has come' and that it can offer solutions to many of the process difficulties that appear inevitable when managers and union representatives seek to resolve difficult issues using cooperative as opposed to adversarial methods. We have set out in detail an IBB model that has won wide support and usage in the U.S. over the last 20 years.

INTEREST-BASED BARGAINING TO DATE

There are a number of conclusions that we can reasonably come to on the basis of what we know about IBB in the U.S. and Ireland. These are that:

- Awareness of IBB among management and union negotiators is stronger than ever before in the U.S. and it is beginning to grow in Ireland
- IBB is being used more widely than ever before in both private and public sector settings in the U.S. and there is some evidence of adoption in Ireland
- IBB has not proved to be a passing fad from the 1980s in the US.
- It has been shown that interest-based approaches can be used in local problem solving around workplace change issues involving local managers, employees and union representatives in both Ireland and the U.S.
- It has also been shown in the U.S. that IBB can be used in major contract negotiations involving traditional bargaining teams made up of senior industrial relations executives and full-time union officials
- IBB can be adapted, as in 'modified traditional bargaining', to suit parties that don't want to or that don't think that they have the capability to use the complete interest-based sequence

- It appears to work best in both Ireland and the U.S. where management and unions are already working cooperative such as through partnership structures and processes
- It seems to emerge in a natural way as a possible response to some of the process limitations associated with loosely structured, dialogue based partnership meetings
- It provides a more robust structure and set of procedures than these conventional partnership meetings.

As Ireland faces increasing competition in world market places, increasing numbers of management and union representatives, especially in organisations with some form of partnership, are likely to see IBB as an attractive option which identifies unions and management as partners who, working together, are capable of facing down their 'enemy outside'.

What current factors, then, are likely to help the wider adoption in Ireland of interest-based bargaining or problem solving?

HELPING FACTORS

We know that for change of a significant order to take place there general-ly has to be a strong 'felt need' to act as a stimulus to new thinking about how things are presently done. The reason for this is that bringing about changes to the status quo carries inherent risks. Parties are unlikely to take such risks unless they are convinced that not changing will be more painful than changing. We have already seen that where there have been com-pelling reasons for management and trade unions to change the way they 'do business' these reasons tend to arise within the competitive environ-ment of companies and in the case of public service organisations from political and public pressures.

There are a number of factors likely to help in the dissemination of awareness around interest-based approaches and in their adoption. Firstly, the factors driving change generally are unlikely to abate for the foreseeable future thus ensuring an ongoing 'felt need' within many organisations.

Secondly, the inherent limitations of the adversarial model are likely to become more exposed over time as parties become more aware of the necessity to find effective means of jointly addressing serious problems and more aware of the alternatives available to them for doing so. It is difficult, for example, to envisage managers deciding to extend employee and trade union involvement into areas such as strategic plans for the future through adversarial bargaining, given the way that it operates. It is far more likely that this would happen through a less adversarial approach.

 Thirdly, there is the leadership work that is being done by various agen-cies to promote the use of 'alternative dispute resolution' mechanisms. Given its role and influence, the Labour Relations Commission is clearly of paramount importance in this area. We have already seen that many of its approaches to dispute resolution are grounded in interest-based principles. Its new strategy statement commits it to increasing its knowledge and understanding of new forms of dispute prevention/resolution in other coun-tries and assessing whether these are suitable for adaptation to the Irish context. Where parties are using cooperative approaches to bargaining and problem solving and where they then bring ensuing differences to the LRC it will be important that the LRC can offer parties the use of processes that are compatible with these cooperative approaches.

Also important is the work of the National Centre for Partnership and

Conclusion

Performance which has sponsored significant research into ways of shapping employment relationships such that they have positive outcomes for organisations and their employees. The ongoing work of partnership bodies such as LANPAG and HSNPF in the local government and health sectors will prove important to the extent that it can generate credible examples of the application of interest-based bargaining and problem solving to significant issues in these sectors. Such examples can influence the thinking of wider numbers of managers and union representatives within and beyond these areas.

Fourthly, there is the crucial influence of management and trade unions. We have seen that managers have choices as to how to shape the relationships with employees and trade unions. Notwithstanding the encouragement of government, employers and trade unions there are many cases where managers appear to favour a reduced or no role at all for trade unions. For managers to be convinced of the benefits of cooperation they need to be convinced, as we saw earlier, that the benefits will outweigh the costs. Reviews of partnership provide evidence from both private and public sectors that this can indeed be the case.

We have seen that in the U.S. the union approach, in the main, has been to stick in so far as possible with the adversarial bargaining approach and to shift when there was little option to do otherwise. In Ireland, as we have seen, trade unions have been to the forefront in arguing the case for partnership at national and workplace levels. They have supported innovations in the areas of information, consultation and joint problem solving.

Most recently, SIPTU has been to the forefront in commissioning information and training workshops on IBB for full-time officials in the health sector where there is a strong drive towards adoption of interest-based problem solving. Other trade unions have also shown interest in this area. There is every reason to believe, therefore, that where management are willing to experiment with interest-based approaches that their trade union counterparts will respond positively.

FINAL WORDS

The interest-based bargaining process is not a panacea. It is a better bargaining process but it requires hard work to learn and do well. In using the process, there will be times of discouragement and frustration.

When this happens, the parties have the advantage of having developed a relationship that supports them in openly discussing their difficulties. This means they should be able to avoid 'the blame game' associated with adversarial bargaining.

Negotiators who become adept in interest-based approaches, will be positioned to represent the interest of those who have entrusted issues to them for resolution, in a more effective way than negotiators whose only available tool is adversarial bargaining.

GLOSSARY OF KEY TERMS

Adversarial collective bargaining This is the traditional 'them and us' type of bargaining or negotiation associated with low trust industrial relations.

Alternative Dispute Resolution or ADR ADR refers to ways of settling disputes that avoid using the courts. Examples are mediation, facilitation, negotiation and arbitration.

Brainstorming Brainstorming is a structured group process for generating ideas in a free and open manner using a flip chart to record the ideas as they are being called out.

Caucus meeting This happens when a bargaining team asks for a break to consider something privately, also called 'side meeting'.

Collective bargaining Collective bargaining is a negotiation process used in unionized employments through which management and trade unions settle issues such as the pay and conditions of employment of employees. The two main types of collective bargaining are 'positional' and 'interest-based'.

Consensus decision making Everyone supports the decision even through it may not be their first choice.

Distributive bargaining A term that is used to describe positional or adversarial bargaining.

Federal Mediation and Conciliation Service (FMCS) The US equivalent to the Labour Relations Commission in Ireland. They train management and union negotiators in the interest-based method and also facilitate such negotiations.

Idea charting Writing ideas on the flip chart so that they become the property of the group and not any one individual.

Industrial relations	Industrial relations refers to the relationships between managers, employees and trade unions and the structures and processes used by them to discuss and resolve issues.
Interests	The underlying needs, wants, concerns that a party has around an issue that needs to be resolved. Term is used typically in IBB.
Integrative bargaining	Another term used to describe interest-based bargaining.
Issues	These are the topics for discussion in negotiations.
Joint problem solving	This term is used here to refer to a variety of ways in which managers, union representatives and employees work together to solve problems. Strictly speaking, adversarial bargaining is a form of joint problem solving but the term is usually used to denote forms of problem solving such as interest-based bargaining and others that are different from adversarial bargaining.
Labour-management cooperation	A term used in the US to describe different forms of cooperation between management, unions and employees in the workplace. Frequently used interchangeably with 'partnership'.
Labour Relations Commission (LRC)	Statutory body charged with helping parties to resolve industrial disputes through conciliation or mediation rather than arbitration (which is the preserve of the Labour Court). Also charged with responsibility for the promotion of good industrial relations.
Options	Possible solutions to a problem. In IBB, they are generated through brainstorming in response to interests that the parties are trying to satisfy.

Partnership	A loose term used to describe different forms of cooperation (information exchange, consultation, joint problem-solving, joint decision making) between managers, union representatives and employees.
Positions	One party's solution to a problem. Typically used in positional bargaining.
Positional bargaining	A term that is used to describe distributive or adversarial bargaining.
Power	The means through which parties influence each other in adversarial bargaining.
Social contract	Term used to describe the nature of the overall relationship between managers, union representatives and employees. In adversarial relationships the social contract is low trust and arms length. In partnership it is based on cooperation to achieve mutual gains.
Standards	Criteria used to decide which options should form the basis of a settlement or solution in interest-based bargaining or problem solving. Using standards is an alternative to using power.
Tentative agreement	Before the parties sign off on a final agreement they reach tentative agreements around an issue or number of issues. The agreement is tentative in the sense that nothing is agreed until everything is agreed.
Voluntarism	Where employers and trade unions are largely free to regulate their own affairs with a minimum of intervention from government or governmental agencies, an industrial relations system can be described as voluntarist.
Win-win bargaining	Another term for interest-based bargaining where the aim is to ensure that the interests of all parties are satisfied to the maximum extent.

REFERENCES

Bacharach, S.B. and Lawler, E.J. (1981): *Bargaining, Power, Tactics and Negotiations,* San Francisco: Jossey-Bass Publishers.

Barrett, J.T. (1996): *A Successful Model for Interest-Based Collective Bargaining and Partnering in the Public Sector,* LRP Publications.

Barrett, J.T. (1998): *PAST Is the Future: A Model for Interest Based Collective Bargaining that Works,* 5th Edition, Washington: Jerome Barrett and Sons Publishing Co.

Barrett, J.T. and Barrett, J. (2004): *A History of Alternative Dispute Resolution: The Story of A Political, Social and Cultural Movement,* San Francisco: Jossey-Bass Publishers.

Bean, R. (1994): *Comparative Industrial Relations: an introduction to cross-national perspectives,* London: Routledge.

Blake, R.R., Shepard, H.A. and Mouton, J.S. (1964): *Managing Intergroup Conflict in Industry,* Houston: Gulf Publishing Company.

Brock, J. and Lipsky, D.B. (eds) (2003): *Going Public: The Role of Labour-Management Relations in Delivering Quality Government Services,* Champaign, IL: Industrial Relations Research Association.

Brommer, C., Buckingham, G. and Loeffler, S. (2002): 'Cooperative Bargaining Styles at FMCS: A Movement Towards Choices', *Pepperdine Dispute Resolution Law Journal,* Malibu, CA: Pepperdine University School of Law.

Chamberlain, N.W. (1951): *Collective Bargaining,* New York: McGraw Hill.

Cohen-Rosenthal, E. and Burton, C. (1987): *Mutual Gains: A Guide to Union-Management Cooperation,* New York: Praeger.

Cooke, W.N. (1990): *Labour-Management Cooperation: New Partnerships or Going Around in Circles?* Michigan: W.E. Upjohn Institute for Employment Research.

Cutcher-Gershenfeld, J. (2003): 'How Process Matters: A Five-Phase Model for Examining Interest-Based Bargaining', in Kochan, T.A. and Lipsky, D.B. (eds), *Negotiations and Change: From the Workplace to Society,* Ithaca: ILR Press.

Cutcher-Gershenfeld, J. and Kochan, T.A. (2004): 'Taking Stock: Collective Bargaining at the Turn of the Century', *Industrial and Labour Relations Review,* Vol. 58, No. 1.

Department of Health and Children (DoHC) (2002): *Action Plan for People Management,* Dublin: DoHC.

Duffy, K. (2005): *Shaping the Future: The Explosion in Labour Legislation,* Presentation to Industrial Relations News Conference.

Ferner, A. and Hyman, R. (1994): *New Frontiers in Industrial Relations,* Oxford: Blackwell.

Fisher, R. and Ury, W. L. (1983 edition): *Getting to Yes: Negotiating Agreement Without Giving In,* London: Penguin Books.

Federal Mediation and Conciliation Service (FMCS) (2002): *Interest-Based Bargaining Workshop Training Manual Presented by Jeanne Frank and John Wagner,* Washington: FMCS.

Federal Mediation and Conciliation Service (FMCS) (2004): *The 2004 National Project on Mediation Approaches to IBB Economics,* Washington: FMCS.

Fonstad, N.O., McKersie, R.B., Eaton, S.C. and Kochan, T. A. (2004): 'Interest-Based Negotiations in a Transformed Labour-Management Setting', *Negotiation Journal,* Vol. 20, No. 1.

Government of Ireland (1997): *Partnership 2000,* Dublin: Stationery Office.

Government of Ireland (2003): *Sustaining Progress,* Dublin: Stationery Office.

Gunnigle, P., Mc Mahon, G.V. and Fitzgerald, G. (1995): *Industrial Relations in Practice,* Dublin: Gill & Macmillan.

Gunnigle, P., Morley, M., Clifford, N and Turner, T (1997): *Human Resource Management in Irish Organisations: Practice in Perspective,* Dublin: Oak Tree Press in association with the Graduate School of Business University College Dublin.

Hastings, T. (2003): *Politics, Management and Industrial Relations: Semi-State Companies and the Challenges of Marketisation,* Dublin: Blackhall Publishing.

Health Services National Partnership Forum (HSNPF) (2004): *Tools for Change Through Partnership,* Dublin: HSNPF.

Healy, S. (2000): *The Partnership in Action at Enterprise Level Project: Independent Evaluation Report,* Dublin: IBEC/ICTU.

Heckscher, C.C. (1996): *The New Unionism: Employee Involvement in the Changing Corporation,* Ithaca: ILR Press.

Human Resources Development Canada (HRDC) (1998): *Evaluation of the Labour-Management Partnerships Programme,* Montreal: HRDC.

Irish Business and Employers' Confederation (IBEC) (1998): *Guidelines for the Development of Partnership in Competitive Enterprise,* Dublin: IBEC.

Irish Congress of Trade Unions (ICTU) (1995): *Managing Change: Review of Union Involvement in Company Restructuring,* Dublin: ICTU.

Irish Congress of Trade Unions (ICTU) (1997): *Partnership in the Workplace: Guidelines for Trade Unions,* Dublin: ICTU.

King, M. (2005): *The Demise of Voluntarism,* Presentation to Industrial Relations News Conference.

Kochan, T. A., and Dyer, L. (1976): 'A Model of Organisational Change in the Context of Labour-Management Relations', *Journal of Applied Behavioural Science,* Vol. 12, No. 2.

Kochan, T.A., Katz, H.C. and Mower, N.R. (1984): *Worker Participation and American Unions: Threat or Opportunity?* Michigan: W.E. Upjohn Institute for Employment Research.

Kochan, T.A., Katz, H.C. and McKersie, R.B. (1986): *The Transformation of American Industrial Relations,* Ithaca: ILR Press.

Kochan, T. And Osterman, P. (1994): *The Mutual Gains Enterprise,* Boston, MA: Harvard Business School Press.

Kolb, D.M. and Williams, J. (2000): *The Shadow Negotiation: How Women Can Master the Hidden Agendas That Determine Bargaining Success,* New York: Simon and Schuster.

Labour Relations Commission (LRC) (2005): *A Quality Shift in Employment Relations: Labour Relations Commission Strategy 2005-2007,* Dublin: LRC.

Lazes, P. and Savage. J. (1997): 'New Unionism and the Workplace of the Future', in Nissen, B. (ed): *Unions and Workplace Reorganisation,* Michigan: Wayne State University Press.

Local Authorities National Partnership Advisory Group (LANPAG)(2003): *Deepening Partnership in Local Government: Strategic Plan 2003-2005,* Dublin: LANPAG.

Local Authorities National Partnership Advisory Group (LANPAG)(2005): *Handling Significant Change through Partnership,* Dublin: LANPAG.

Locke, R., Kochan, T. and Piore, M. (1995) (eds): *Employment Relations in a Changing World Economy,* Cambridge: The MIT Press.

Martin, R. (1992): *Bargaining Power,* Oxford: Oxford University Press.

McKersie, R.B. (1996): 'Labour-Management Partnerships: US Evidence and Implications for Ireland', *Irish Business and Administrative Research,* Vol. 17, 1-13.

McKersie, R.B., Eaton, S.C. and Kochan, T.A. (2004): 'Kaiser Permanente: Using Interest-Based Negotiations to Craft a New Collective Bargaining Agreement', *Negotiation Journal,* Vol. 20, No. 1.

Murphy, T.V. (1997): 'The Resolution of Industrial Disputes' in Murphy, T.V. and Roche, W.K. (eds), *Irish Industrial Relations in Practice: Revised and Expanded Edition,* Dublin: Oak Tree Press in association with the Graduate School of Business University College Dublin.

National Centre for Partnership and Performance (NCPP) (2002): *Modernising Our Workplaces for the Future: A Strategy for Change and Innovation,* Dublin: NCPP.

National Centre for Partnership and Performance (NCPP) (2003): *Achieving High Performance: Partnership Works – The International Evidence,* Dublin: NCPP.

National Centre for Partnership and Performance (NCPP) (2004(a)): *The Changing Workplace: A Survey of Employee's Views and Expectations,* Dublin: NCPP.

National Centre for Partnership and Performance (NCPP) (2004(b)): *The Changing Workplace: A Survey of Employers' Views and Expectations,* Dublin: NCPP.

National Centre for Partnership and Performance (NCPP) (2004(c)): *Information and Consultation: A Case Study Review of Current Practice,* Dublin: NCPP.

National Centre for Partnership and Performance (NCPP) (2005): *Working to our Advantage: A National Workplace Strategy,* Dublin: NCPP.

O'Donnell, R. and Teague, P. (2000): *Partnership at Work in Ireland: An Evaluation of Progress Under Partnership 2000,* Dublin: Department of the Taoiseach.

O'Dowd, J. (1998): *Employee Partnership in Ireland: A Guide for Managers,* Dublin: Oak Tree Press.

O'Dowd, J. (2002): *If It Ain't Broke – Fix It Anyway: How Partnership Can Help Improve Industrial Relations,* LRC Journal, Vol. 1.

O'Dwyer, J.J., O'Dowd, J., O'Halloran, J. and Cullinane, J. (2002): *Partnership in the Civil Service: A Formal Review,* Dublin: Department of Finance.

O'Hanlon, R. (1976): *Joint Consultation in Irish Industry,* Dublin: Irish Productivity Centre.

Roche, W.K. (1996): *The New Competitive Order and the Fragmentation of Employee Relations in Ireland*, Working Paper, Dublin: Centre for Employment Relations and Organisational Performance, Graduate School of Business, University College Dublin, Blackrock, Co Dublin.

Roche, W. K. (2002): 'Whither Partnership in the Public Sector?' *Administration*, Vol. 50, No.4.

Roche, W.K. and Gunnigle, P (1995): 'Competition and the New Industrial Relations Agenda' in Gunnigle, P. and Roche, W.K. (eds), *New Challenges to Irish Industrial Relation,* Dublin: Oak Tree Press in association with the Graduate School of Business University College Dublin.

Roche, W.K. and Turner, T. (1998): 'Substitution, Dualism and Partnership: Human Resource Management and Industrial Relations', in Roche, W.K., Monks, K. and Walsh, J. (eds), *Human Resource Management in Ireland,* Dublin: Oak Tree Press in association with the Graduate School of Business University College Dublin.

Roche, W.K. and Geary, J.F. (1998): *'Collaborative Production' and the Irish Boom: Work Organisation, Partnership and Direct Involvement in Irish Workplaces,* Working Paper, Dublin: Centre for Employment Relations and Organisational Performance, Graduate School of Business, University College Dublin, Blackrock, Co Dublin.

Rojot, J. (1991): *Negotiation: From Theory to Practice,* Portland, Oregon: International Specialized Book Services.

Rubinstein, S.A. and Kochan, T.A. (2001): *Learning from Saturn,* Ithaca: ILR Press.

Schein, E.H. (1999): *Process Consultation Revisited: Building the Helping Relationship,* Reading, MA: Addison-Wesley.

Schwartz, R.M. (1994): *The Skilled Facilitator: Practical Wisdom for Developing Effective Groups,* San Francisco: Jossey-Bass Publishers.

Services Industrial Professional Technical Union (SIPTU) (1999): *Participation and Partnership in Changing Work Organisation,* Dublin: SIPTU.

Stepp, J. and Barrett, J. T. (1990): 'New Theories on Negotiations and Dispute Resolution and the Changing Role of Mediation', Bureau of National Affairs, *Daily Labour Reporter:* Washington D.C., January 17, 1990.

Stepp, J.R., Sweeney, K.M. and Johnson, R.L. (2003): 'Interest-based Negotiation: An Engine-Driving Change', *The Journal of Quality and Participation,* Sept/Oct. 1998.

Teague, P. (2004): *New Developments in Employment Dispute Resolution,* Dublin: Labour Relations Commission.

Telecom Eireann/Trade Union Alliance (TE/TUA) (1998): *District and Local Partnership Training Manual by Boyle and Associates,* Dublin: TE/TUA.

Totterdill, P. and Sharpe, A. (1999): *New Work Organisation in Ireland: Report of the Independent Evaluator,* Dublin: Irish Productivity Centre.

Turner, T., and Morley, M. (1995): *Industrial Relations and the New Order: Case Studies in Conflict and Cooperation,* Dublin: Oak Tree Press in association with the Graduate School of Business University College Dublin.

Ury, W.L, Brett, J.M and Goldberg, S.P (1988): *Getting Disputes Resolved: Designing Systems to Cut the Costs of Conflict,* San Francisco: Jossey-Bass Publishers.

Von Prondzynski, F. (1995): 'Ireland: Between Centralism and the Market' in A. Ferner and R. Hyman (eds) *Industrial Relations in the New Europe,* Oxford: Blackwell.

Walton, R.E and McKersie, R.B (1991 edition): *A Behavioural Theory of Labour Negotiations,* Boston: ILR Press.

Walton, R.E, Cutcher-Gershenfeld, J.E. and McKersie, R.B. (1994): *Strategic Negotiations: A Theory of Change in Labour-Management Negotiations,* Boston, MA: Harvard Business School Press.

Ware, J.P. (1980): *Bargaining Strategies: Collaborative versus Competitive Approaches,* Harvard Business School Teaching Note 1, 9-480-055.

Weiss, D.S. (1996): *Beyond the Walls of Conflict: Mutual Gains Negotiating for Unions and Management,* Chicago: Irwin Professional Publishing.

Woodworth, W.P. and Meek, C.B. (1995): *Creating Labour-Management Partnerships,* Reading, MA: Addison-Wesley.

ISBN 1-41206318-3